Praise for *Get Naked*

"*Get Naked* is excellent! So easy to read, to the point, and practical. Derek's humor gives you a chance to laugh at serious issues like finances, while absorbing effective lessons to get you on the right track. Want unity and communication in your marriage? *Get Naked!*"
- **Shaunti Feldhahn, National Speaker and Bestselling Author of *For Women Only* and *For Men Only***

"Derek delivers his guidance practically, straight-up, and with two feet planted in reality. Don't let your marriage become a statistic – put the tools in these pages to use and enjoy the ride!"
- **John G. Miller, author of *QBQ!, Flipping the Switch,* and *Outstanding!***

"Finally. Financial advice newlyweds desperately need paired with enough wit and humor to help the medicine go down. Taking this book seriously is going to keep a lot of marriages out of the therapy office and thriving in an area where so many couples miss it."
- **April Miller, Marriage Counselor and host of Life Unleashed Radio**

"Money can be a source of tremendous tension in marriage. In his book, *Get Naked*, Derek Sisterhen teaches us not only how to handle our finances but ultimately how to better handle our marriage. *Get Naked* is a must read whether you are on the same page financially or need help getting there, the strategies included in this book will take your marriage to the next level."
- **Tony and Alisa DiLorenzo, Marriage Coaches and authors of *Stripped Down: 13 Keys to Unlocking Intimacy in Your Marriage***

"Derek Sisterhen is a trusted voice in the area of sound money management. In *Get Naked*, he draws from his experience as a financial coach and, more importantly, as a husband, to deliver a vital message with a perfect balance of practicality, humor, and Christian wisdom. I highly recommend this book for all couples in those critical early years of marriage and beyond!"
- **Dustin Riechmann, EngagedMarriage.com**

"If Christine and I had a compass to guide us early in our marriage we could have avoided many arguments. *Get Naked* fills that void and is required reading for any married couple. It's humorous and practical with clear action steps to improve any marriage."
- **Justin Lukasavige, author of *Become a Coach* and host of CoachRadio.tv**

getnaked
stripping down to money & marriage

derek sisterhen

Past Due Press
Raleigh, NC

GET NAKED: STRIPPING DOWN TO MONEY & MARRIAGE

Copyright © 2010 by Derek Sisterhen

International Standard Book Number: 978-0-9825465-1-2

Cover design, artwork, and layout by Christy Knutson, www.christyleeknutson.com.
Editorial assistance provided by Faith Dwight, www.faithdwight.com.

Unless otherwise indicated, Scripture quotations are from:
The Holy Bible, New International Version © 1973, 1984 by
International Bible Society,
used by permission of Zondervan Publishing House.

Where appropriate, names have been changed to protect identities and preserve confidentiality.

Printed in the United States of America.
ALL RIGHTS RESERVED

No part of this publication may be reproduced, stored in a retrieval system, or transmitted, in any form or by any means – electronic, mechanical, photocopying, recording, or otherwise – without prior written permission.

ISBN Information

Get Naked: Stripping Down to Money & Marriage / Derek Sisterhen

ISBN: 978-0-9825465-1-2
1. Family 2. Finance, Personal

To purchase more copies or to inquire about Derek, visit www.getnakedbook.com.

*For my amazing wife, Elisa,
without whom this could not be written.*

*Your love, encouragement, and grace inspire me;
thanks for showing me how to be a giver.*

contents

INTRODUCTION

CHAPTER 1	**1**
Why (In the World) are You Getting Married?	1
The Deck Stacked Against You	4
Money is Not the Problem in Your Marriage	6
CHAPTER 2	**9**
I Think We're Alone Now...	9
Your Designer Set of Baggage	11
A Sisterhen Story	12
CHAPTER 3	**17**
The Loose Cannon vs. The Cheapskate	17
Ch-Ch-Ch Changes	20
Just Comes Natural, I Guess	22
CHAPTER 4	**27**
Let's Talk About (Anything But) Money	27
Dreams, Goals, Sex	29
When Two Become One	31
"We," Not "Me"	35
CHAPTER 5	**41**
Honesty is the Best Policy	41
His & Hers Financial Worksheets	43
What if it's Rough?	52
What if it's Awesome?	55
CHAPTER 6	**59**
Come Together	59
Role Play (I'll be the Fireman, You be the French Maid)	60
Budgeting in the Buff	65
Let's Get it On!	73

contents

CHAPTER 7   **85**
    The Big Picture   85
    God at the Center   91
    Staying Naked   92

AFTERWORD   **97**

APPENDICES   **101**

THANKS   **115**

ABOUT THE AUTHOR   **117**

introduction

I never really thought I'd wind up writing a book about money, much less marriage. There are books aplenty on both subjects (many of which I draw from within). When I started coaching folks toward their financial goals, I realized that I was using a lot of anecdotes and personal experience from earlier in my own marriage to paint pictures – typically (okay, mainly) of what not to do.

When I was engaged to my wife, we went through a premarital counseling course at our church. To be honest, neither of us took it seriously enough to wring out the wisdom we so desperately needed. All Elisa and I were thinking about was the wedding day (or night, as the case may have been for half of us).

I still recall the book we used for the course. Only two questions in the supplemental study guide required us to think of how we'd practically manage money together. Now, that's totally understandable because there are many important issues that need to be addressed between the butterfly-love-struck-rose-petal-filled stares of two engaged people.

Dealing with in-laws, spiritual beliefs, value systems, and deciding whether you'll spank the kids or issue timeouts are all significant –

don't get me wrong.

However...

Research shows that the majority of couples who divorce cite money problems as the cause.[1]

Aha! So, if we'll wrangle with this issue of money, we could essentially divorce-proof our marriages – at least from a financial perspective. Think about it.

I needed some meat and potatoes with regard to managing money in my premarital counseling course. Simply identifying who would pay the bills and who would buy groceries wasn't enough. I didn't know then that I would wind up having a fight with my wife over a $40 pillow purchase – causing her to stomp out of the house in frustration – in the first few months of marriage.[2] I didn't know then that being a budget control freak choked off a vital line of communication in our marriage and actually prevented me from living a fulfilled life with my lovely lady.

If you're engaged right now to the man or woman of your dreams, pause for a second and really let what I'm about to say find its way through the cloud of lace and "Canon in D" and honeymoon plans enshrouding your brain: if you don't get on the same page with your spouse about money, your marriage is doomed.

Plain and simple.

Do not pass *Go*. Do not collect marital bliss.

If you're a newlywed, I need you to fend off the married-life-is-perfect mindset you've been basking in since your wedding day and really let this sink in: if you don't get on the same page with your spouse about money, you'll constantly experience a lack of complete unity.

---

1   2007 Citibank study.
2   Sadly, how to handle a situation like this was not in the study guide.

You've got to get straight on this now before little differences of opinion become huge rifts of separation.

If you've been married for some time, and you're just now realizing how much you have yet to learn, I need you to stop thinking about how he always leaves the toilet seat up or she always leaves the car cluttered with junk, and let what I'm about to say sink in: if you don't get on the same page with your spouse about money, you'll keep from experiencing real intimacy in your marriage. There is no time like the present and no institution like marriage where grace and mercy can rectify previous missteps.

Will it be easy? No.

Will it be worth it? Absolutely!

This book was written as a resource to save your marriage. That's right; I said *save* your marriage. You'll find that relating with your spouse on money matters is not about numbers at all, but about how you express love. We're going to address the financial elements in-depth; I have included a slew of worksheets and exercises to help you do so. But make no mistake; when it comes to establishing goals and developing a plan for accomplishing them, your success will hinge on your willingness to elevate your spouse's needs above your own.

That is what you've entered into. Serving your spouse in this way will make managing money a breeze.

Plus, you'll probably wind up having more sex.

chapter one

"When two people are under the influence of the most violent, most insane, most illusive, and more transient of passions, they are required to swear that they will remain in that excited, abnormal, and exhausting condition until death do them part."

-George Bernard Shaw

why (in the world) are you getting married?

It all seemed like such a logical progression[1] of events to me:

There's a proposal.

There's an engagement ring.

There's registering for gifts at all sorts of retailers (making sure that extended family members living across the country have access to

---

1   "Logical" and "marriage" are antonyms. I don't think anyone who gets engaged really knows what they're getting themselves into. If we did, we'd immediately go to therapy after the popping of The Question. And we'd stay there until our wedding day.

the stores where we identified the perfect hand towels).

There's securing photographers, reception sites, limousines, caterers, DJs, bands, processional music, recessional music, a honeymoon location, and a bridal party.

There's making sure future in-laws are satisfied in the process.

There's signing up for a premarital counseling class.

All of this happens before we even sign the marriage license.[1]

We tend to exaggerate the wedding process, making The Wedding Day out to be the defining moment of two lives. Some folks take months, or even years, to plan their moment of matrimony, only to experience a *blurring* sensation as the whole event unfolds.

"Was that Uncle John or Cousin Suzie who just shook my hand?"

"Is "The Electric Slide" on a loop? I think I've only heard two other songs in the last four hours."

"I remember walking down the aisle and cutting some cake and getting on a plane and now I'm sunburned... I think we had a lot of fun in Cancun."

Now, please don't make me out to be a jaded wedding pessimist. I love a wedding just as much as the next guy. Heck, I've even gotten misty-eyed at a few of them. However, if The Wedding Day was the defining moment of our lives, we'd have very little else to live for.

Direct from *my* premarital counseling book, *Saving Your Marriage Before it Starts*, Drs. Les and Leslie Parrot say, "The truth is most engaged couples prepare more for their wedding than they do their marriage. More than one million copies of bridal magazines are sold each month, focusing mainly on wedding

---

1 If you've made it all the way through the engagement adventure, congratulations! If not, read Philippians 3:13.

ceremonies, honeymoons, and home furnishings – but not marriage itself."[1]

When I ask, "Why are you getting married?" I'm really asking if you know what you're getting yourself into. Even the Apostle Paul wrote about single people enjoying their singleness because, "those who marry will face many troubles in this life, and I want to spare you this."[2]

Whoa! You "will face many troubles"? But everything is supposed to be perfect in marriage, isn't it?

Derek, we're completely in love! My heart races when he's around! I can't wait to spend the rest of my life with him. Every emotional ounce of me is oozing with love for him and I know he feels the same way!

Talk like this can't help but bring the famous *Jerry Maguire* scene to mind.[3] You know the one: when Jerry tells Dorothy, "You complete me." It's amazing. It's beautiful. It's love!

It's a movie.

While I believe that God draws two people together whose strengths can balance out each other's weaknesses – and I've experienced it firsthand myself – we have to be very careful to enter into marriage with two feet planted firmly in reality.

"Those who marry will face many troubles in this life."

When we see our spouses for who they really are we can offer them grace and mercy.

---

1 According to a 2006 review by the Merchanti Chronicle, the annual revenue of the wedding industry currently tops $100 billion and the average cost of weddings has doubled since 1990 to $27,000.
2 1 Corinthians 7:28.
3 The notoriety of this scene overshadows my personal favorite: the "Who's Coming with Me?" scene.

We can encourage them.

We can laugh with them.

We can cry with them.

We can give them love even when they don't deserve it.

Just like Jesus.

the deck stacked against you

Recently I overheard a TV program about weddings cite that some people are changing the traditional vow language to say "as long as our love shall last" instead of "until death do us part." The problem is that the "in love" feeling so many of us operate under dissipates after about two years.[1] One of the most difficult lessons to learn in life is that true love is not a feeling.

It's a choice.

Before you say *I do*, there is a vital point that must be understood. The institution of marriage is under attack in our culture. There was a time when "until death do us part" actually meant you stayed with your spouse until one of you kicked the bucket. Today, 40% of first marriages end in divorce. Around 60% of second marriages disintegrate. A full 75% of third marriages do not make it.[2] Regardless of which marriage this is for you, statistically your *best* odds for survival are focusing on making the current one work.

In his book, *The Five Love Languages*, Gary Chapman unveils the power behind choosing to love your spouse. "If love is a choice, then [we] have the capacity to love after the 'in-love' obsession has died and [we] have returned to the real world. That kind of love

---

1 Psychologist Dr. Dorothy Tennov has conducted numerous long-range studies on the "in love" phenomenon.
2 The Five Love Languages, page 35.

begins with an attitude – a way of thinking. Love is the attitude that says, 'I am married to you, and I choose to look out for your interests.'"[1]

The challenge we face so often in our culture is breaking away from a me-centered existence. Especially in marriage, being me-centered will undermine any hope of growing in deep intimacy with your spouse. As a matter of fact, that's what makes marriage inherently counter-cultural: we're supposed to lift our spouse's needs above our own.[2]

Jesus spoke of this kind of sacrificial love: "My command is this: Love each other as I have loved you. Greater love has no one than this, that he lay down his life for his friends."[3]

Romantic media – film, TV, music, etc. – leads us to believe that *feeling* in love is essential for love to last. Fairy tales remind us over and over again of how destined lovers overcome incredible odds to live *happily ever after*.[4] The only trouble is that Prince Charming has morning breath, and the princess wakes up with terrible bed-head.

We must choose to love each other.

How about when the prince tells the princess to stop buying so many pairs of glass slippers because, if she doesn't, they'll have to build a new castle with more closet space? And then, after saying this, the prince goes out and buys a big screen, flat panel TV to watch the upcoming jousting tournament?

Or, because the princess was raised by a local peasant, she only buys generic products at the village market in order to save money. Meanwhile, the prince thinks generic products are of poor quality; he'd rather spend more for the best brands.

---

1   The Five Love Languages, page 36.
2   Ephesians 5:22-25.
3   John 15:12-13.
4   "We have been poisoned by fairytales." –Anais Nin

Or, the prince is committed to putting the royal offspring in private school, regardless of cost, because he thinks it's better for their long-term education and development. Meanwhile, the prince and the princess are having trouble making the mortgage payment on the castle...

money is not the problem in your marriage

With the exception being those who experience truly unforeseen financial hardships (think medical emergency), there's an easy explanation for the vast majority of couples with financial problems:

The way they behave.

Make no mistake: you choose the way you behave with money. Sure, based on a variety of factors, you'll have a predisposition toward certain behaviors, but ultimately you choose how money enters and exits your individual economy.

In the world of personal finance, about 20% of your success is related to head-knowledge and understanding financial mathematics. The other 80% of your success is rooted in what you see when you look in the mirror.[1]

It's you, in all your glory.

In Matthew 6:21, Jesus said, "For where your treasure is, there your heart will be also." According to Him, you reveal your value system through your handling of money. I can learn who you are simply by reading your checkbook or online banking register. The way you behave with money tells me plenty about your mental, emotional, spiritual, and relational states of being.

In your marriage, relational behavior is most commonly displayed by how you communicate with your spouse. Premarital counseling

---

[1] The Total Money Makeover, page 4.

focuses extensively on helping engaged couples understand each other's communication style. (If you're engaged and haven't signed up for premarital counseling, I highly recommend it. When two different people come together in marriage, they bring plenty of baggage and back-story that will influence their future behaviors.[1])

I haven't met any married couples that set out with the objective of allowing their communication to slowly disintegrate. However, good intentions are sometimes lost in the execution. More often than not, the couples I work with who are struggling financially cannot tell me the last time they talked about their long-term financial goals. They typically *can* tell me the last time they fought over money matters.[2]

Are you committed to serving your spouse and elevating his or her needs above your own?

How do you show love to each other?

Where do you want to be a year from now? How about 20 years from now?

How do you communicate together?

What do you know about each other financially?

It's time to be open and honest. You're agreeing to spend the rest of your life together, so honesty is a pretty good place to start.

You're going to see each other naked, you know.

---

1 Scott Stanley's 2006 Journal of Family Psychology research reported couples who receive premarital education have a 31% lower chance of divorce.
2 Which was probably when they were in the car on the way to see me.

get naked

chapter two

"If you ask couples before they're married if they think money will be a big problem, most will say no. They might as well be saying, 'We're not worried about money. We'll be livin' on love.'"

-Authors Robert Wolgemuth & Mark DeVries

i think we're alone now...

When the dust settles after the pomp and circumstance of the engagement, The Wedding Day, and the honeymoon, we're left with two people who have to figure out the best way of doing life together.

Now, that's an undertaking.

As newlywed creatures of habit, we tend to slip back into the routine that served us well prior to getting married. But our habits and routines don't always jive with those of our new spouse.

I neatly rolled the toothpaste tube from the bottom; Elisa pinched in the middle.

After dinner, I rinsed dishes and left them in the sink. Elisa rinsed and put them in the dishwasher.

I got ready – from shower, to shave, to hair styling, to tooth brushing – completely naked.[1] Elisa showered, dried off, and robed herself before anything else.

I collected receipts from every place I spent money, kept them in chronological order, reconciled them with monthly bank statements, stapled them to the statements, and kept them in a binder for long-term archiving.

Of the receipts Elisa actually had, some stayed in the dark recesses of her purse for months, others were thrown into a large box (where she also kept birthday and Christmas cards from years past).

The rose-colored glasses slowly lift from our eyes during those first few months of marriage and the real spouse comes into plain view.

The progression reminds me of the show *The Crocodile Hunter*, when Steve Erwin would track down wild animals in Australia and wait for them to emerge from their hiding place. First we'd see the leaves rustle or the surface of the water would slightly break and ripple. Then there would be the crocodile, or hippopotamus, or shark for all to see.

Steve would always say, "Isn't she a *beaut*?!"

The Drs. Parrot say, "Marriage is filled with both enjoyable and tedious tradeoffs, but by far the most dramatic loss experienced in a new marriage is the idealized image you have of your partner."[2]

Expecting two different people to approach money in the exact same way is expecting way too much. You come from different backgrounds and have had different financial experiences leading

---

1 It's true – not even a towel around the waist. I love to air-dry. "Get Naked" applies to more than just money.
2 Saving Your Marriage Before it Starts, page 22.

up to this point in your life.

So, if as a wife you couldn't wait to spend Sunday afternoons pouring over budget spreadsheets with your new husband...

If, as a husband, you couldn't wait to make your first big purchase – a fishing boat – with your new wife...

...you may have an idealized image of your partner regarding money.

your designer set of baggage

At some point in your dating relationship, you probably recognized that your future spouse was raised in a unique family culture.[1] This culture has direct implications on how your future spouse will do many things:

1. Handle Money
2. Raise children
3. Participate in the household
4. Plan for the future
5. Interact with you

In *The Most Important Year in a Man's Life*, Robert Wolgemuth and Mark DeVries discuss the impact of your family culture as you begin managing money with your new spouse:

> "If your parents argued about money, that was normal for you. If your dad paid the household bills because he didn't trust your mother with the checkbook, that was normal. If your dad "surprised" your mother with new cars; if your mother went shopping like it was a daily sport, even when she didn't need anything; if your parents lived with heavy credit card debt; if your parents tried to hide their

---
[1] I say "unique" to imply "different," not to imply "weird;" although "weird" may be more accurate.

expenditures from each other; if your parents always waited until they could pay cash before they bought something – all of these things were normal for you. You're bringing them into your marriage as standard equipment."[1]

Depending on the nature of and your ability to reckon with your upbringing, we refer to any lingering personal dysfunction as "baggage." The good news is that as long as you're a human being with a pulse, you'll have baggage. This means your spouse has it, too, and that's just fine. You both have strengths that will compliment each other's weaknesses and discovering those will usher forth lots of growth and lots of laughs.

As we moved through our engagement, I told Elisa that some of my baggage was motivating me to give my all to our marriage. My parents divorced when I was two years old. Both were remarried some years later – my mom when I was five, my dad when I was seven. I have grandparents who've been divorced, remarried, divorced, and remarried. I have aunts and uncles who've have been divorced and remarried. I have step-aunts and step-grandparents that have been divorced and remarried. My family tree looks more like a family shrubbery.

My commitment to Elisa was that when I said "until death do us part" I actually meant that I would walk through fire before giving up on our marriage. I've unfortunately witnessed way too much relational destruction and I didn't want to perpetuate it. Nevertheless, this baggage definitely influenced – and continues to influence – me in my marriage.

a sisterhen story

I took a job in the banking world after I completed my undergraduate degree in Business Administration. Prior to getting married, my job took me to a small North Carolina town where I

---

[1] The Most Important Year in a Man's Life, pages 99-100.

rented an apartment. As a single guy living alone, I had generally low personal overhead.[1] My monthly grocery budget was about $80.

Then I got married.

Elisa moved into my, ahem – excuse me – *our* apartment when we returned from the honeymoon. She found herself smack dab in the middle of a town where she knew no one, without a job lined up, and me around *every* morning and evening. This was a major life change and it occurred in the blink of an eye.

Since I spent my days at an office 25 minutes away, I didn't know that my bride was slowly slipping into depression. Her degree in Health Policy and Administration would have been extremely attractive in the health care job market around Raleigh, but we lived just outside a military town where those positions were limited. Cabin fever was setting in. I didn't know then that one way to deal with depression is to spend money.

I started coming home from work to meals Elisa saw prepared during her daily Food Network fix. All of the sudden we were eating gourmet – and spending a lot of money to do so. It wasn't uncommon for one meal's ingredients to cost half of what I used to spend in an *entire month* on groceries.

Pretty soon we had a financial problem on our hands.

the pillow fight

One day I came home from work to find Elisa sitting on the couch watching TV.[2] The couch was different, though. I was used to seeing the navy blue upholstery contrasting with the stark white apartment walls every day, but now there were splashes of color all over it. Vibrant pillows stood out against the solid blue.

---

1 You'd be amazed how long I can go on PB&J!
2 Food Network fix.

"What do you think?" she asked, waiting anxiously for me to share her enthusiasm.

"Hmm..." I trailed off. Nothing I could say would sound very enthusiastic, so I stood silent and motionless. She tried to explain where she got them, but all I saw were dollar signs.

I don't really recall anything either of us said after that, but it wasn't good. We have the ability of finding the most biting, insensitive words when arguing with the ones we love. The only thing I do remember was how that fight – our first real one in three and a half years of dating and three months of marriage – ended.

She walked out the door.

The pillows cost $40.

I was stunned. My marriage was ending over $40.

Shortly after walking out, Elisa called me and asked me to come down to the parking lot of our apartment building. She was in her car still smarting from our fight, but she wanted me to accompany her as she drove around town blowing off steam. That afternoon I learned how dangerous my mouth could be; I also learned how to shut up.[1]

Here's what was really going on: Elisa was looking for any outlet possible to nurture her desire to nest and be productive during the day. For me, I kept mental score of every $40 gourmet meal, $20 magazine rack, $15 vase, and $10 pillow and believed that these expenses would undermine our ability to reach our savings goals.[2]

The truth was that neither of us knew how to relate to each other financially when we started our marriage. We both operated as though we were still single because I figured she saw everything my way and she figured I saw everything her way.

---
1 Will Rogers said, "Never miss a good chance to shut up."
2 They were really my savings goals that Elisa knew nothing about.

The first step to resolving the situation was to get back to common ground. We had to remind each other that we loved and cared for each other deeply, and that our marriage mattered way too much to let financial problems get the better of us so soon. We had to go back to the drawing board and discover what our priorities and passions were. In short, we had to get to know each other again...

...financially speaking.

get naked

chapter three

"For the love of money is the root of all kinds of evil. Some people, eager for money, have wandered from the faith and pierced themselves with many griefs."

-1 Timothy 6:10

the loose cannon vs. the cheapskate

How would you describe your financial personality? Have you ever thought about it – that you have a *financial* personality type?

It won't come as a surprise to you which two words line up at opposite ends of the financial personality type spectrum:

Saver and Spender.

You can determine your financial personality type with relatively high accuracy by honestly answering this question:

> *If I found $100 in my pocket, what would I do?*

"I'd buy groceries because I just spent my last $100 on video games and Twizzlers."

"I'd use $50 to buy a new book and a shirt I've had my eye on; the other $50 I'd save for later."

"I'd invest 95% of it in a portfolio of large and small cap mutual funds, and 5% in a money market account for capital preservation. Assuming an average annual return of 10%, this asset allocation strategy will yield a net gain of $5,270 in 40 years!"[1]

With responses like these, it should come as no surprise that alternative terminology has been developed to describe financial personality types:

Cheapskate and Loose Cannon.[2]

We already discussed that your disposition to saving and spending money has roots in your upbringing. Now, let's understand that the financial personality traits occur on a continuum. You're not completely a saver or completely a spender. In order to preserve peace and build unity in your marriage, you need to identify where you fall on the continuum and understand where your spouse falls, along with how he or she perceives *your* financial personality type.

First, let's dip our toes in the minds of savers: what they think of themselves, and what they think about spenders.

Savers view themselves as methodical, organized, and economical. There is a process in place and they intend to follow it. The process is this:

Work, make money, put money in bank account.

Work, make money, put money in bank account.

---

1 Seriously? Take your spouse out to dinner and a movie (don't talk about money), then come home and have sex.
2 Want to tick off a saver? Call him or her a "cheapskate".

Work, make money, put money in bank account.

Retire.

Spend some of the money.

Die.

They assign value to what they will enjoy *at some future date* as a result of their disciplined savings regimen.

Savers tend to perceive spenders through a certain lens: reckless, overindulgent, and materialistic. To demonstrate their holiness and self-righteousness, they'll make Biblical references like Proverbs 6:6-8, "Go to the ant, you sluggard; consider its ways and be wise! It stores its provisions in summer and gathers its food at harvest."[1]

Now, for the other side of the proverbial coin let's look at spenders. Spenders view themselves as enthusiastic, giving, and spontaneous.[2] There is a process in place for spenders, too:

Work, make money, spend money.

Work, make money to catch up because too much money was spent earlier, spend money.

Work, make money to catch up because too much money was spent earlier, spend money.

Work.

Die.

They assign value to what they can enjoy *now* as a result of their

---

1   Savers will fling the "you sluggard" part in the general direction of spenders when citing this verse.
2   For many savers, the word "spontaneous" sounds like the noise Flipper makes. Over and over and over.

hard work.

Spenders also have a particular perspective on savers: rigid, stingy (ergo, cheap), and reluctant. They'll spiritualize their spending personality with scriptures like James 4:13-14, "Now listen, you who say, 'Today or tomorrow we will go to this or that city, spend a year there, carry on business and make money.' Why, you do not even know what will happen tomorrow."

Eat, drink, and be merry, for tomorrow we die![1]

So, in identifying where you fall on the continuum, what benefits and drawbacks do you see in your life as a result of your financial personality type?

What are some opportunities for growth as you relate to your spouse?

ch-ch-ch changes

According to a *Money* magazine poll, 84% of husbands and wives say money is the primary source of tension in their marriage, expressed mainly by clashes over spending and saving. This finding isn't all that surprising. What *is* surprising is that there isn't even a close second.

Occasionally, we get this notion that when we're married we'll be able to change our partner. That somehow they'll see the light and leave their old, *ridiculous* ways of doing things behind.[2] A little Counseling 101 tells us that we can't change anybody; they must want to change and make the change for themselves.

In *QBQ: The Question Behind the Question*, John Miller says, "Change *only* comes from the inside, as a result of decisions made

---
1 Check out the Dave Matthews Band classic, "Tripping Billies."
2 Like getting ready completely naked…

by the individual."[1]

Why would anyone want to change? Simple: if it's in their best interest to do so. If productive communication, unity, and intimacy in your marriage are in your best interest, **YOU** must make changes.

Sounds like humility.

On the saver-spender continuum, I'm a saver. Very few interests of mine cause me to lose control and spend.[2] However, if you ask Elisa what she got when we first were married, she'd tell you Ebenezer Scrooge, Jr.

Elisa is a spender. She loves spending on visual stimulation: paintings, antique furniture, interior decorations, clothing, and international travel. She also loves giving freely to help others. When I married her, I realized that even though Elisa wouldn't use credit cards to live beyond her income, she could still spend a pretty penny.

This makes a Scrooge nervous.

In the wake of the Pillow Fight, Elisa and I were opening up to the idea that changing from the old way of doing things would benefit us. I showed her what just a little bit of money saved each month could grow to by the time we hit retirement age.

Did you know that if you invest $400 a month at a 10% average annual return over a 40-year career, it grows to more than $2.5 million?

You can get a lot of visual stimulation with that kind of cash!

She then told me about her desire to give money in support of our missionary friends and our church. After making room for it in our

---
1   QBQ: The Question Behind the Question, page 68
2   My Achilles heel is music, whether recorded music or new accessories for my guitar and drum set.

budget, I began to discover the tremendous joy you can have by passing money along to bless others.

I was willing to change and Elisa was willing to change. Without her I wouldn't have a life; without me she wouldn't have a retirement.

just comes natural, i guess

Turns out, men and women are different.[1]

Aside from your financial personality type, we truly cannot go much further without acknowledging how you and your spouse are uniquely wired as you approach money. Understanding a few natural tendencies will definitely help you know your spouse in a deeper way and make sense of some specific behavioral tendencies.

men

Ladies, you need to know something about your men. In spite of a culture that is critical of the traditional establishment of the man as the household leader, in spite of a workplace welcoming women to higher and higher rungs on the corporate ladder, in spite of your ability to generate income, your man feels *a burden* to provide for his family.

In her groundbreaking study *For Women Only*, Shaunti Feldhahn found that nearly eight out of ten men would still feel a compulsion to provide for their families, even if their wives earned enough to support the family's lifestyle.[2] "For most men the drive to provide is so deeply rooted that almost nothing can relieve their feeling of duty."

Further, 71% of men said that "the responsibility to provide is

---
[1] Some experts say we even come from different planets, which really explains a lot about women, if you ask me.
[2] For Women Only, page 77.

always or often on their mind." Surprised, ladies? It's the real deal. But guess what? Your man actually *likes* this burden!

Providing for his wife is a man's natural way of demonstrating his love for her. When a man is providing, he feels powerful and he feels depended on.

He feels valuable.

Don't worry, darling; I'll take care of you.

And because most men have an innate fear of failing those around them, they will do whatever is necessary to take care of their families.

women

Men, your ladies are beautiful creations provided by God to help and support you.[1] Because of this, and in spite of a popular culture that paints women as recreational shoppers bent on keeping up with the Joneses, your woman is more concerned with the security of your *relationship* than financial security.

Shaunti's husband Jeff helped her with a follow-up study, *For Men Only*. In it he writes, "For her, 'emotional security' matters most: feeling emotionally connected and close to you, and knowing that you are there for her no matter what."

In fact, when faced with choosing between two negative situations – either financial problems or struggles arising from insecurity (lack of closeness) in their marriage relationship – a full 70% would rather endure financial problems. "And women who described themselves as [currently] struggling financially were even *more* likely to prefer emotional security!"[2]

One woman even said, "Feeling secure and close in the relationship

---
1 Genesis 2:18.
2 *For Men Only*, page 77.

is so much more important, it's not even part of the same discussion as work or money."

The tendency for most men is to go into hyper-provider mode when life gets tough. Don't let your natural desire to provide crowd out nurturing the most important earthly relationship you have.

Now, I'm not saying that your woman doesn't appreciate financial security. As a matter of fact, financial security is very important to most women. Making risky decisions that could severely impact your family will drive a deep and disastrous wedge in your relationship.

Foster ongoing dialogue with your wife about your perspective on work, money, and life together. Let her know that she matters.

You married her because she matters.

the naked truth

Tim and Lindsey came to me after more than ten years of marriage. They couldn't talk about money without resorting to major tongue-lashings. Though Tim made great money, they were still up to their ears in debt and needed a plan to get out.

Lindsey called me in tears about two weeks after our first session and said that Tim was still openly blaming her for their difficult situation. She told me that even though they both made poor financial choices in the past, what she really wanted was to reconnect with her husband emotionally. I encouraged her to sit down with Tim that evening, apologize for her part of the mistakes, and then tell him that she was committed to working through this with him because that was the only way out of their mess.

When we met three weeks later for another session, both of their countenances were different – almost tranquil. A burden had been lifted from the back of the relationship. They weren't fighting against each other now; they were fighting against the financial situation – together.

We've wrapped up who you are and how you're naturally wired. Let's start stripping down to money and marriage.

get naked

chapter four

"If a husband and wife are not communicating about finances, I'll guarantee you that they're not communicating about anything."

-Larry Burkett

let's talk about (anything but) money

Outside of recognizing that marriage is God's creation[1], and having Him at the center of it, the most critical element for success between a husband and wife is communication.

Blah, blah, blah.[2]

That's what we always hear, isn't it? That marriage is all about communication? There are whole sections in bookstores devoted to marriage and probably 90% of the books in them deal with communication. All this communicating makes for a pretty impressive industry.

---

1   Genesis 2:18-25.
2   Note: This is not a form of good communication.

The truth is that if you can't figure out how to effectively communicate in your marriage, your boat will sink before you leave the harbor. Seriously, this is what actually causes marriages to fail, not money.

When couples communicate well, they understand each other's needs, wants, and desires. They understand fears, hopes, and dreams. Communication is what cultivates intimacy. Intimacy prevents people from spending money without talking it over first.

Or making life decisions without their spouse's input.

Truly, good communication is the key to your marriage working. And when you communicate well, effectively managing your money *together* becomes second nature because it's in your very best interest to do so.

Sadly, for many married couples, talking about money is like talking to impassioned protestors – even if you agree with them, there will still be yelling.[1] Many times when couples argue over money, each spouse will have deeply felt convictions about what they *want* to be done, but are unwilling to really hear what the other spouse is trying to say so they can get to what *needs* to be done.

In Ephesians 4:29, Paul says, "Do not let any unwholesome talk come out of your mouths, but only what is helpful for building others up according to their needs." That means there's no room for attacking your spouse, making digs or passive-aggressive remarks, and undermining an environment of unity. You do this often enough and you'll find yourselves having awkward conversations about who brought in the mail simply because you won't be able to talk about anything else.

---

[1] "Marriage is one long conversation, checkered by disputes." –Robert Louis Stevenson

dreams, goals, sex

The tendency for most folks is to put the cart before the horse when it comes to managing their finances. A Harvard study found that over 80% of Americans like the *idea* of setting goals for their lives, but they don't actually follow through and set them. The same study found that those who write down their goals accomplish *ten times more* than those who don't, on average.

During an engagement and early in marriage, the romance flows so generously that it's impossible not to dream huge dreams. The difference between *dreams* and *goals* is relatively small, but in practice it's gigantic.

A *dream* is something strongly desired or that will fully satisfy. A *goal* is a dream with a plan of action and timeline for completion. That means that if you want to take a trip to Venice with your spouse and make out on a gondola while the gondolier sings *That's Amoré*, you have to determine how and when you'll make that happen.

When will you go?

Have you researched airfares and accommodations?

What will you have to save between now and then to pay for the trip?

How will this impact your monthly household budget?[1]

In order to put your best foot forward in your marriage, you must get on the same page with your spouse. Start with the *Dreams & Goals* exercise.

---

[1] If you don't want to answer questions like these for the dreams in your life, just remember that "normal" means accomplishing 90% LESS than you could have (Harvard MBA Goals Study).

dreams & goals

Think about what you want life to look like based on the following time thresholds. Will you have emergency savings in place in the next year? Will you pay off your debt? Will you buy a house? Will you want to put your children in private school? Will you travel internationally?

Complete the following worksheet separate from your fiancé or spouse. Plan a date night, lay the two pages down side-by-side, and have some fun discussing your dreams and goals.

dreams & goals

In the next:	I want to achieve:	This will cost:	To do this, we must:
12 Months	• • •	• • •	• • •
24 Months	• • •	• • •	• • •
Five Years	• • •	• • •	• • •
Ten Years	• • •	• • •	• • •

The *Dreams & Goals* exercise is a very practical way of taking two different sets of opinions, thoughts, goals, and dreams and synthesizing them into something cohesive. My guess is that you found many similarities between the two separate lists. There may have been differences based on your timelines for completion – like your wife wants the commercial-grade cotton candy machine in five years while you really want it in the next 12 months.

Typically, couples who perform this exercise will find that the majority of their dreams and goals match up when they compare worksheets. It's no surprise, really. You got married because you liked each other and held certain interests and beliefs in common. That will carry over into what you intend to do with your money. And in order to bring any of the items on your lists from paper to reality, you both must become united in your efforts.

When you learn your spouse's dreams and goals, you will get a glimpse of his passions and his heart.

That sounds like intimacy to me.[1]

Growing intimacy and respect for each other will lead to one very important place: the bedroom.

So, do I even need to tell you?

Get naked![2]

when two become one

The whole idea of two people becoming one has mesmerized us for thousands of years. Ancient Greek storyteller Homer wrote, "There is nothing nobler or more admirable than when two people who see eye to eye keep house as man and wife, confounding their enemies and delighting their friends."

Seeing eye to eye in a marriage may be a stretch for some[3], but that

---
1 The Dreams & Goals exercise was Elisa and my first step to communicating clearly and productively about money (without boxing gloves and mouth guards).
2 If you aren't married yet, go home and take a cold shower.
3 "Eye for an eye" might be more accurate.

doesn't change the miracle of synergy that results when two people join together as one. Given the state of contemporary marriages, two unique personalities in a living arrangement requiring they dwell in the same shelter and stay faithful to each other is just as noble and admirable today as it was in Homer's time.

And if we can get these two individuals to pay bills together, well, they're regular royalty!

From the very beginning, the Bible says, "For this reason a man shall leave his father and mother and be united to his wife, and they will become one flesh."[1] The financial implications of this one verse are huge!

Two become one.

From *The Five Love Languages*: "At the heart of mankind's existence is the desire to be intimate and to be loved by another. Marriage is designed to meet that need for intimacy and love. That is why the ancient biblical writings spoke of the husband and wife becoming 'one flesh.' That did not mean that individuals would lose their identity; it meant they would enter into each other's lives in a deep and intimate way."[2]

Thankfully, we don't lose our identity when we marry. In fact, the refining process we undergo as husbands and wives in a productive, intimate, loving marriage means that we are going to become better versions of ourselves. In order to experience this, though, we must fully yield to our partner and to cultivating an atmosphere of intimacy in our daily lives.

intimacy in practice

I was teaching a workshop to a group of about eighty people some time ago. I asked, "Do you and your spouse have separate checking accounts?" With an audience that size, I can easily see who is

---
1 Genesis 2:24.
2 The Five Love Languages, page 22.

quickly stealing uncomfortable glances at each other. An older lady in the crowd was staring down her husband.

I tried to make it seem like I hadn't seen the lady, but before I knew it I was looking right at her and asking, "Why?" The answer, more often than not, is that they don't trust each other with money.

Another excuse I often hear is that one or the other's parents "always did it that way."

Ever think of *why* they did it that way?

I don't believe you can experience the profound pleasure of true intimacy that God desires for your marriage by operating from separate bank accounts. This is a hard pill for some to swallow, particularly those from older generations.

Earlier we discussed what Jesus said about the relationship between your treasure and your heart. When we're told that marriage unites two people and they become one, but then those two people manage their "treasure" separately, have they truly become *one flesh* in their hearts?

In 1 Corinthians 7:4 Paul says, "The wife's body does not belong to her alone but also to her husband. In the same way, the husband's body does not belong to him alone but also to his wife."

Now, it just so happens that this verse is all about sex and how married people shouldn't withhold it from each other. But here's what stands out to me: our bodies are our most important physical assets on planet Earth. If we don't take care of them, the story's over because we're dead.

Why in the world would Paul say that we are to live in such a relationship to our spouse that our bodies don't even belong to us anymore? It's because this is the ultimate sign of commitment.

That at my most basic level – skin, bones, spirit – I don't belong to myself anymore.

And yet, I will exclude from that most sensual and holy form of commitment anything that has to do with *my* money, right?

Because it's *mine*, you see.[1]

I want to sleep with you, but the idea of sharing a checkbook kinda freaks me out. I mean, do I really even know you yet?

Just like when we give ourselves to our spouse physically, when we combine our finances we enter into a deep trust agreement. We trust our spouse to act tenderly and with honor, so that all future decisions about money will be made together.[2]

And, as *one flesh*, to act in my best interest means to act in my spouse's best interest. With trust rooted this deep, your intimacy will grow and flourish, regularly reminding you that you made the right choice by giving everything you have to your spouse and also serving as relational insulation when the challenges of life come.[3]

The other reason two must become one with money is to compel communication. If you manage your money separately, your financial conversations will be reduced to who needs to write a check to whom to cover the electricity bill.[4]

Besides, what was the point of the *Dreams & Goals* exercise if you aren't going to manage together the resources that make the dreams and goals reality?

You know what else disrupts intimacy in a marriage? "A lack of intimacy can also be traced to a lack of spiritual vitality. One study

---

1   If you're always focused on "mine," get used to having "yours" alone.
2   There are exceptions for financial infidelity; please read Appendix 4: What About Abuse?
3   And they *will* come.
4   It'll feel great when you see that first book of checks with both of your names printed on them, I promise!

showed that spirituality ranked among the six most common characteristics of strong couples," found the Drs. Parrot in *Saving Your Marriage Before it Starts*.[1]

As the old saying goes, "The couple that prays together stays together."

Marriage is the hardest job you will ever have. Seeking guidance, direction, peace, patience, grace, mercy, and the will power to keep from occasionally throwing your spouse out of a moving vehicle from the One who created you and everything else builds "spiritual vitality."

You will need prayer because managing money with your spouse will not always be easy. But from the moment you commit yourself to your bride or groom, you are committing to *join* her or him on the journey.

You're in it together as *one flesh*.

"we," not "me"

A few months before I got married, I went out to lunch with Caleb, one of my best friends. Caleb married another great friend of mine a year earlier and so our lunch conversation turned toward life after *I do*.

I try to absorb as much as I possibly can from those who've gone into uncharted waters ahead of me – especially when they say they've made mistakes. What struck me then was when Caleb said it took getting married to realize how selfish he could be.

Selfish? I remember thinking. *How is that possible?*

I never thought Caleb was selfish at all; it seemed like he was always

---

[1] Saving Your Marriage Before it Starts, page 48.

looking out for everyone else's needs instead of his own.[1]

Naturally, this scared me as I inched closer to my wedding with the dawn of each new day. If Caleb – *of all people* – realized he was selfish in marriage, then I was going to be stricken with a realization of my own narcissism so thick I'd have to cut it with sheep shears.

Now that I've been married awhile, I understand what he meant. It's not a matter of constantly forcing my way of thinking on my wife, but rather a mentality and heart condition.

Do I look to serve myself first?

The *Dreams & Goals* exercise is important because it allows for dialogue. It allows you to see what is important to your spouse. This exercise is not intended to be a once-and-done activity. Time will pass and goals will change. Some will be accomplished. Some will become less important. So revisiting and updating the list together is critical.

Let's say you and your spouse had a great date night, using the *Dreams & Goals* exercise to establish what you desire to accomplish together. If you then proceed to go off like a loose cannon, electing to "forget" the goals and go your own way, you should expect negative consequences.[2]

Your relationship will be strained.

You will look like a liar (you said you wanted to do *this*, but then you went and did *that*).

It's simply not worth the fleeting satisfaction you get from buying something in secret, without your husband's knowledge.

Or justifying an outrageous purchase without first discussing it with

---

[1] As a matter of fact, if he and I had a run-off, I would surely win the selfishness election.
[2] Give Fleetwood Mac's "Go Your Own Way" a listen; great song.

your wife.

Want to lose the respect of your spouse and begin the slippery slope toward divorce? Don't honor your goals with your lover.

When you revisit your spouse's goals, you stay acquainted with the passions and desires of his or her heart. Those passions and desires move to the top of your mind. You begin to think less about how *you* can do whatever *you* want and more about how *we* can accomplish great things together.

If you think this is unfulfilling, wait until you see the look on your lover's face when you check off a goal that was on her list. Remember, marriage is counter-cultural because it's built on the foundation of elevating your spouse's needs above your own.

it shall persist!

We'll talk about having your short-term goals handy when preparing monthly budgets in a little while, but at a minimum you should revisit your goals with your spouse each year. I recommend doing it around November as you plan for the year ahead.

But what happens when you're in a rough spot? Maybe the financial wheels have fallen off the wagon or something unexpected happens that throws a major wrench in your plans. What if you hit a relational rut and are finding yourself *choosing* to love a whole lot more than *feeling* love?

Three doctors performed a study of 9,000 marriages – 3,000 of which resulted in divorce – and found an interesting theme: "There may be nothing more important in a marriage than the determination that it shall persist. With such determination, individuals force themselves to adjust and to accept situations which would seem sufficient grounds for breakup, if continuation of the marriage were not the prime objective."[1]

---

1 Saving Your Marriage Before it Starts, page 49.

The study's results confirm the concept of "we", not "me", because if we all acted out of our own self-interest, we'd see divorce filings even higher than their current levels. No one likes relational stress. No one likes tension and having awkward conversations about who brought in the mail. No one likes the idea that they aren't reaching their own goals in life as quickly or as smoothly as hoped.

No one likes divorce.

Commit to selflessness and persistence in your marriage. Establish a common set of goals after completing the *Dreams & Goals* worksheets and discuss the best method for reaching them by the timelines you've determined.

And don't forget to *celebrate* together as you begin crossing different items off the list.

Be *creative*...[1]

---

1 If it isn't clear enough, I mean celebrate naked.

dreams and goals sample

In the next:	I want to achieve:	This will cost:	To do this, we must:
12 Months	Emergency savings Living room furniture Pay off credit card 1st Anniversary trip to California	$2,500 $1,500 $900 $1,000	Work on a monthly spending plan; pull back on going out to eat; open a savings account
24 Months	Pay off student loan Save for house down payment Save for retirement Prepare to start a family	$5,000 $15,000 $400/mo	Develop solid monthly spending plan; prioritize saving over spending; pay extra on debt
Five Years	Take a trip to Hawaii Purchase a car with cash Save for kids' college New bedroom suite	$3,500 $9,000 $250/mo $1,500	Build solid planning and saving foundation today to prepare for these goals; cut out smaller vacations for one larger trip
Ten Years	Family vacation: cruise Save for kids' college Purchase a boat Private school option	$4,000 $250/mo $15,000 $400/mo	Become and stay debt free; plan each month's expenses; teach kids how to handle money wisely

get naked

chapter five

"Facts are stubborn things; and whatever may be our wishes, our inclinations, or the dictates of our passions, they cannot alter the state of facts and evidence."

-John Quincy Adams

honesty is the best policy

If I had a dollar for every time I heard my mother say, "Honesty is the best policy," I'd probably have about $350.

How many TV shows, movies, theatre productions, and real life examples can you think of where couples that lie to each other do more harm than good?

A lot.[1]

---

1 I imagine a team of television show writers sitting around a table saying, "What's the next episode going to be about?" Then one of them says, "Oh! I know! What if Ted lies to Marsha about buying the old Corvette then tries to hide it from her!" You've seen that episode a hundred times on a hundred different shows, haven't you?

Unfortunately, life is not like a sitcom or romantic comedy. Lies aren't always resolved at the end of a 30-minute episode or 90-minute film.

Some of us have past financial baggage that we aren't too proud of and the idea of telling our man or woman about it is a bit daunting. When it comes to talking about your financial past with your fiancé or spouse, honesty isn't just the best policy.

It's the *only* policy.

John Miller says, "Personal accountability is about each of us holding *ourselves* accountable for our own thinking and behaviors and the results they produce."[1]

Taking responsibility and being accountable for our actions is another unpopular concept in our culture. We're much better at passing the buck or pointing the finger of blame elsewhere. Getting naked means we have to rethink this strategy.

Honor your spouse with honesty.

Even if it hurts.

the naked truth

I still vividly remember meeting Matthew for the first time. In our consultation he explained that he'd only been married to Molly for six months before she found out about his excessive spending behind her back.[2] He put thousands of dollars in new purchases on credit because he wanted to prove that he could provide anything she desired.

The outcome was devastating. Because of his deception, she was

---
1 QBQ: The Question Behind the Question, page 64.
2 Important Note: This couple was working with a professional marriage counselor as I helped them financially.

on the verge of leaving him for good.

They had only been married for *six months*!

Remember, men, relational security is more important than financial security to most women. When you spend money in secret or lie about where you got the funds for purchases, you deliver a huge blow to the relational security gland in your wife.

Ladies, if you make purchases without telling your husband, you're tearing down the respect he so greatly craves and, with your actions, you're telling him, "You can't give me what I want."

his & hers financial worksheets

Perhaps you received his and hers paraphernalia for your wedding.[1] My guess is no one gave you a great set of matching spreadsheets and said, "Have at it! Experience financial unity!"

Consider this next part my wedding gift to you.

the money maker

Where does your money come from?

Do you work a primary job and a part-time job?

Are you self-employed?

Do you receive child support or alimony?

Do you receive income from investments?

Getting naked about your income is step number one in having an honest conversation with your spouse or fiancé about your financial

---
1 Does it really get much better than matching flannel robes?

situation. Take a moment to complete the *Naked Income Sources* worksheet.

naked income sources

Source	Amount	Pay Frequency
Salary 1		
Salary 2		
Salary 3		
Self-employment		
Bonuses		
Child Support		
Investments (Interest, Dividends, etc.)		
Disability		
Social Security		
Unemployment		
Other:		
Other:		

Now that we know where your money comes from, let's talk about what you own and what you owe.

i see you, baby, shaking that asset

Many of the people I meet don't have (nor really want) a basic understanding of accounting. Just so we're all on the same page, I'll explain a couple of concepts for you and then we'll jump in and determine your naked net worth.[1]

In the financial world, an *asset* is not a certain personality trait or characteristic people like about you. Instead, an asset is anything that you own that holds some form of marketable value.

---
1 I trust your spouse believes you to be invaluable, priceless, precious, and other synonyms.

Your house – if you own it – is an asset. So is your car.[1] So is the money in your checking and retirement accounts. The antique china from your Aunt Mable probably counts, too.

Your hair dryer and curling iron are not assets.

Neither is your favorite old, plaid-upholstered recliner that catapults its users when the footrest is retracted.[2]

When you get married all your assets become your spouse's assets, and vice versa. However, some assets don't come unaccompanied.

A *liability* is any money you owe to another party. Could be a mortgage or car loan, credit card balance or student loan. Could be a furniture loan or that "gift" from Cousin Charlie that he's hoping you "give" back.[3]

When you match up what you own with what you owe, you can calculate your personal net worth. Taking the value of an asset and subtracting any liability amount attached to it determines your equity position in that asset – or how much of the asset you actually own. The total of all your equity positions is your net worth.

Assets - Liabilities = Net Worth

In the worksheet on the next page, list out your assets and your liabilities. Make your best guess of what your assets are worth and review recent statements that show balances for liabilities. Keep in mind that credit card, student loan, and personal loan debt falls under "Unsecured Debt," which means you won't have an asset to attach them to.

---

1   But don't get confused. The car is the largest asset Americans buy that goes DOWN in value; the average vehicle loses 70% of its value in the first four years.
2   You may have "been through a lot together." It's still not an asset.
3   Refer to the Appendix discussion "The Borrower is Slave to the Lender-in-Law" about borrowing money from family.

naked net worth

Item	Asset	Liability	Equity
1st Mortgage			
2nd Mortgage			
Vehicle 1			
Vehicle 2			
Cash On Hand			
Checking Account 1			
Checking Account 2			
Savings Account 1			
Savings Account 2			
Money Market Account			
Brokerage Account			
Retirement Plan 1			
Retirement Plan 2			
Stocks & Bonds			
Antiques & Collectibles			
Boats & Other Vehicles			
Unsecured Debt (negative)			
IRS Debt (negative)			
Other:			
Other:			
TOTAL			

The figure in the lower right-hand corner of the worksheet is your net worth. Don't be disappointed if it seems low or even negative. In a situation where your net worth is negative, you owe more than the value of your assets. About 25% of American households have a negative net worth, so you're in good company.[1]

Just not the kind of company you want to keep.

---

1 U.S. Department of Commerce.

consumer debt: i and owe and you[1]

When you woke up this morning, you joined a world where the typical family of four is confronted with at least 1,500 advertising and marketing messages each day.[2] You joined a world where at least six billion credit card offers are sent out annually (that means over 16.4 million offers will be mailed today).

You joined a world where every marketer wants you to say *Yes!* to their product, then let you worry about paying for it on your own time.[3] So we have deals like 90 days same-as-cash, no interest and no payments for three years, 0% financing, and on and on.

By *consumer debt* I'm talking about any credit devices that have enabled you to purchase a product or service you otherwise wouldn't have been able to purchase. I include credit cards, vehicle loans, personal loans (money owed to family or friends), retail loans (like loans on furniture and electronics), and student loans.[4]

Consumer debt is typically unsecured. The exception is the vehicle loan – whether for your car, boat, four-wheeler, or Segway.[5] We treat mortgages differently because real estate has a track record of increasing in value. Your car, living room set, and even your Segway begin declining in value the moment you take them home.

In the worksheet below, list your consumer debts by debt type. Indicate the balance on the loan, the monthly minimum payment, and your interest rate.

---

1 Check out The Avett Brothers song "I and Love and You."
2 Fordham University College of Business Administration marketing study.
3 We don't want those little details to get in the way of a sale, you know.
4 Some folks argue that student loans are considered more of an "investment". Investment or not, it's still a liability that you must repay no matter how much your earning potential increases after graduation.
5 I'm shaking my head as I consider the notion of making payments on a Segway.

naked consumer debt

Debt Type	Outstanding Balance	Minimum Payment	Interest Rate
Credit Cards			
Retail Loans			
Vehicle Loans			
Personal Loans			
Student Loans			
TOTAL			

We'll discuss the best method for paying off your debt shortly. For now, use this worksheet as a tool to organize your debts and share them with your fiancé or spouse.

monthly spending exposed

Back in Chapter 1 we talked about Jesus' no-nonsense comment in Matthew 6:21, "For where your treasure is, there your heart will be also."

Jesus calls us on the carpet in love by linking our treasure and the condition of our hearts.

Since honesty is the best policy, it's time you were honest with yourself by writing all your monthly expenses on paper. Now, I've worked with enough people to know that most folks have only a foggy idea of their expenses. This next worksheet will allow you to get very specific as you define your monthly outgo.

We'll talk about creating an actual budget with your spouse a little later. In order to do that, though, you'll need to identify all the places money flows to in your world. You may need to get a couple of recent bank statements to determine how much you spend in the categories listed below. In the "Non-Monthly Expense" column, list any amounts you pay on an irregular basis (i.e. insurance premiums paid quarterly, homeowner's association dues paid annually, etc.) Then indicate when each Non-Monthly Expense is due in the "When Paid?" column.

naked monthly expenses

Spending Category	Monthly Amount	Non-Monthly Expense	When Paid?
Giving			
Savings			
Emergency Savings			
Other Savings			
IRA Contributions			
Self-employment Taxes			
Housing			
First Mortgage/Rent			
Second Mortgage			
Home Repairs/Maintenance			
Homeowner/Renter Insurance			
Real Estate Taxes			
Homeowner's Association			
Pest Control/Lawn Care			
Utilities			
Electricity			
Water			
Gas			
Cable/Phone/Internet			
Trash/Sewer			
Mobile Phone			
Security System			
Food			
Groceries			
Eating Out			
Transportation			
Car Payment 1			
Car Payment 2			

Spending Category	Monthly Amount	Non-Monthly Expense	When Paid?
Other Vehicle Payment(s)			
Fuel			
Repairs/Oil/Tires			
Auto Insurance			
Registration/Inspection			
AAA/Roadside Assistance			
Personal Needs			
Clothing			
Personal Care/Hair Care			
Other Insurance			
Disability Insurance			
Health Insurance			
Long-term Care Insurance			
Life Insurance			
Prescriptions/Co-pays			
Other Spending			
Birthday/Wedding Gifts			
Christmas Gifts			
Childcare/Tuition			
Entertainment			
Vacation/Travel			
Walkin' Around Money			
Subscriptions			
Memberships			
Other:			
Other:			
Other:			
Other:			
TOTAL			

So, how does it look? Was this the first time you listed all of your monthly spending? Were there any categories that surprised you when you totaled up your expenses? As we build toward creating a combined set of worksheets for you and your spouse, your awareness of your own spending will help you develop a realistic budget together.

Now that you have your own set of financial worksheets we can dig a little deeper. We need to look in the mirror again and understand how we'll approach the numbers on those pages with our spouse.

what if it's rough?

Just like physically getting naked with each other, exposing your financial condition to your spouse can be overwhelming the first time around. There could be past mistakes that you or your spouse (or both of you) are still paying for.

So, what if one or both of you are in rough financial shape?

who wants to say grace?

Beginning conversations about money with prayer is an excellent way to focus your hearts and minds on God and allow His grace to penetrate the situation. This should also remind you both of the critical requirement – yes, it's required – to extend grace to each other.

Colossians 4:6 says, "Let your conversations always be full of grace." Grace doesn't mean you have to look past the trouble spots in your partner's finances and pretend they aren't there. Grace means that you recognize that you aren't perfect, your partner isn't perfect, and that you'll love him or her in spite of the situation. You must forgive your spouse of any past or current financial mistakes that impact you. You also must hold your spouse accountable to a new financial standard that leads to deeper unity in your marriage and your relationship with God.

So, pray before you talk about money and "let your conversations always be full of grace."

debt-whacked

When you look at your Naked Net Worth and Naked Consumer Debt worksheets, you'll see all the debts outstanding. You must understand and accept that any debt your fiancé has will become your debt when you say *I do*. That means that a portion of your income will be devoted to paying off your spouse's debt in marriage.[1]

First, seek to understand where the debt came from. Was it a lack of understanding about how debt works? Was there an emergency situation and borrowing was the only option at the time? Was it unbridled spending? Don't judge, just understand.

Second, learn what your spouse wants to do about the debt. Debt in a marriage can become a big, ugly deal, so we're going to devote substantial time to it a little while later. For now, though, grow deeper in your knowledge of your spouse by learning where he or she wants to go with his or her debt.

my upkeep is my downfall

Remember when you were eight years old and you asked your parents for a new bicycle and they'd give you that skeptical look? The one that says, *"If we knew you were going to cost us so much we wouldn't have brought you into this world."* And then they'd say, "What? Do you think money grows on trees?"

And then, when you turned eighteen, you were bombarded with credit card offers and you realized that money doesn't have to grow on trees because the mailman delivers other people's money (OPM) to the mailbox? And then, because you had "money," you went and bought the bicycle your parents didn't buy for you? But, because you really wanted it ten years earlier, it didn't do anything to fill the

---
[1] Two become one, baby! Your mess is my mess, let's clean it up together!

void in your heart (and garage), so you went back out and bought a big screen television, surround sound system, and 58 DVDs?

Remember?

Well, your parents were right: money doesn't grow on trees. And OPM comes at a price (called interest).

Contentment is a spiritual issue with financial implications. Here's what the Bible says: "But godliness with contentment is great gain. For we brought nothing into the world, and we can take nothing out of it. But if we have food and clothing, we will be content with that."[1]

Perhaps you and/or your spouse have confused wants with needs in the past. Recognize that your upkeep can truly become your downfall if you don't regulate your expenses. Again, we live in a marketing culture that begs us to say *Yes!* so we must view our expenses with an understanding that *stuff* doesn't equal long-term satisfaction.[2]

For young newlyweds in particular, there is a tendency to attempt to recreate the lifestyle they were used to when they still lived with their parents. They'll overextend themselves to get into a larger house, to take bigger vacations, and to buy better stuff. The problem is their parents had 20 to 30 years to construct that lifestyle. It can't be reconstructed in the first 24 months of a new marriage without the use of debt and excessive spending.

the naked truth

Mark and Natalie were a textbook example of a young couple attempting to keep pace with their parents' standard of living. They bought a huge house that came with a huge mortgage right out of the gate; almost 50% of their take-home income went toward their

---
1   1 Timothy 6:6-8.
2   If it did, we'd have no reason to buy new and improved stuff.

monthly payment.[1] They also couldn't say "No" when friends invited them on lavish vacations.

Even though they made a great income for a young couple, nearly every dollar that came in the door was thrown right back out the door because they couldn't control their spending. Upon realizing that their lifestyle owned them and prevented them from reaching their long-term family planning and retirement goals, they reassessed what contentment truly meant for their marriage.

Ultimately, they sold the house, put boundaries around their spending, and began aggressively paying off over $50,000 in student loans. They aren't letting previous mistakes nor pressure from others around them result in poor financial decision-making that would hamper their relationship.

what if it's awesome?

First, let me congratulate the 1.79% of you who fall in this category. Kudos![2]

Second, don't get complacent.

I've seen many couples who've done wise things financially make a slow shift into neutral. When difficulties are easily identifiable we can quickly come up with a set of objectives like paying off debt, building up some savings, contributing to a retirement plan, etc. But once all the to-dos are checked off, you'll need to create a new list.

Fostering good, regular dialogue about where you stand is critical at all times, but may be even more so when times are good. If productive communication isn't an ongoing habit, you can be in for a real shock if an emergency situation like a job loss or illness

---
1   Check out the Appendix discussion "We Want to Buy a House."
2   1.79% is a sarcastic exaggeration that is not scientifically substantiated. The rest of us normal folks are envious.

strikes.

Make it a point to continue setting goals together and identifying new worthwhile uses for your money. Find creative ways to give to others; do it together to make disciplined giving not only a habit in your marriage, but something you can pass along to your children.

the naked truth

Adam and Carrie were married seven years before I met with them. They had recently relocated to the area with their two kids after living further south. During our first conversation I remember how easily and comfortably they talked to each other about their financial situation. They genuinely liked each other![1]

While their only financial blemish was an outstanding car loan (one that was paid off in a few months), they were struggling to answer the question, "What next?" After seven years of marriage they were becoming listless with their money.

I learned that Adam desired a career transition out of home improvement and into people improvement; he wanted to help others make positive, lasting changes in their lives. With Carrie onboard, we created a strategy that would have them saving for retirement and their kids' college, while also saving extra in their emergency fund for Adam to make his job transition and pursue a career he could be passionate about.

Even if you and your spouse are starting out on strong financial footing, don't miss the opportunities to continue setting goals, talk about what you desire to accomplish together, and invest in your relationship.

Getting naked isn't an event, it's a process.

---
1 Imagine that! Married people who actually like each other!

stripping down to money and marriage

get naked

chapter six

"My lover is mine and I am his..."

-Song of Solomon 2:16

come together

I probably could have called this book *Get Vulnerable*. I didn't – intentionally – because I know more people (perhaps even you) will pick up just about anything pertaining to nudity.[1]

That's what I love about reading Song of Solomon: pretty hot and steamy stuff in that book of the Bible.[2] "My lover is mine and I am his," appears in chapter two as Solomon and his wife give themselves to each other physically. You don't have to read very far to realize that they've already given themselves to each other emotionally and spiritually.

---

1 It's okay to be honest about this; sex sells – you just continue to prove it!
2 Song of Solomon 1:4, "Take me away with you – let us hurry! Let the king bring me into his chambers." Ladies, call your husband 'king' tonight and have him bring you into his chambers (be patient with him as he removes all the decorative pillows you probably have piled on the bed).

Sounds a lot like becoming *one flesh*, doesn't it?

It also sounds like they are completely exposed and vulnerable in front of each other. And in this state they combine their individual selves to form one complete and new body.

When you meld your financial world with your spouse's, understand that you'll both be in a position similar to Solomon and his lover. Maybe you've already spent a lot of time talking about money and what you intend to do financially as husband and wife. Even so, there is something very disarming about spreading out "where your treasure is" on paper, in black and white.

Since you promised each other you'd be around until one of you kicks the bucket, it makes the most sense to establish a productive, inviting method for discussing your financial game plan on a regular basis. As you come together to create and follow through with monthly objectives for your money – whether for the first time or the first *good* time – remember to respect your spouse and show love.

role play (i'll be the fireman, you be the french maid)[1]

In Chapter 5, you laid out your entire financial world. Before we bring it all together with your spouse, we'll need to define exactly what roles each of you will play on a day-to-day, month-to-month basis so you have the greatest opportunity to make the most of your money together.

I'm going to tell you something you need to hear: you aren't perfect and your spouse has certain qualities you'll come to rely on.

The Drs. Parrott says, "There is an inherent completeness when a man and woman marry. Our partner makes up for what we lack. When we are discouraged, they are hopeful. When we are stingy,

---
1 I hope you love that we're talking about role-playing in a book about money as much as I do!

they are generous. When we are weak, they are strong. Because we are male and female joined together, there is wholeness."[1]

Sounds like more two-become-one talk to me.

It can actually be fun determining what role you and your spouse will play in managing your money. If you bring the right amount of lightheartedness into the discussion, you'll find that each of you possess the strengths to fill in for the other's weaknesses.

We're going to play to those strengths – especially when it comes to budgeting.

firemen[2]

Firemen strike me as methodical people. They have a process: the 911 call comes in, they slide down the pole, they jump into their fire suits, they determine the most efficient route to the fire, they plan the best way to get any people out of harm's way, and they effectively extinguish the blaze.

In the world of personal finance, you're a fireman if you get satisfaction or joy from digging into spreadsheets and putting together an effective budget. You like knowing there is a spending structure in place (especially one you created) across which you can distribute your income.

Perhaps you enjoy learning a new Excel formula that will make your budgeting spreadsheets more efficient and one thousand times more impressive (in the eyes of other firemen, of course).[3]

If you are the fireman, you will have very specific financial responsibilities on a monthly basis. You will be required to create

---

1 Saving Your Marriage Before it Starts, page 93.
2 Please note that plenty of women function as the "fireman" in their financial role-play; I just find the word "fireperson" silly.
3 "Fireman" sounds really cool – even sexy; you could also call these people "nerds" if you want.

the first draft of your monthly budget and make any necessary revisions after the actual Role Play.

french maids[1]

I don't think I've ever seen a movie (though I do mainly watch comedies) where a French maid was actually going around a house making beds and cleaning up after the homeowners.

French maids are generally whimsical, free-spirited. In the world of personal finance, you're probably a French maid if you're less interested in how a plan of action is put together and more interested in the expected outcome. Basically, you'd rather put a feather duster to use than put together a monthly budget.

I know what you're thinking: *Derek, what's the point of having a French maid if they don't serve a purpose?*

Au contraire, mon frère (or soeur)![2]

Each partner in a marriage is in tune with different aspects of a monthly budget. For example, men tend to be more aware of mechanical expenses, like car repairs and home maintenance. Women are usually on the front lines of social expenses, like dinner parties with friends and kids' activities.

So a French maid brings that awareness to the Role Play table when the fireman presents the monthly budget. Likewise, the French maid knows that he or she is quite responsible for following through on the budget – and making sure that the fireman is accountable to it, also.

role playing

Once you've determined what role you play, it's time to *actually*

---
1 Please note that plenty of men function as the "French maid" in their financial role-play; you're welcome to dress up, I guess, if you're into that sort of thing.
2 French to English: "On the contrary, my brother (sister)!"

play.

No, no, no...wait! I don't mean *that* kind of *play*...

...yet.

Let's get your budget in place and then you can move on to firemen rescuing French maids and other related activities.

In the last week of the month, the fireman will create the first draft of the coming month's budget. Take your very best estimate of what you anticipate your expenses to be for each expense category.

If you know you're traveling to visit family, put it in there.

If you know you need to get an oil change, put that in there, too.

After completing the first draft of the coming month's budget, the fireman must present it to the French maid. During this time, the French maid must review the plan for the month and provide input:

"Your parents are coming to visit; we'll need to buy extra groceries."

"Is there anything we can do to move more money into our Emergency Fund?"

"The car insurance premium is due next month."

Now, when married people talk at length about money, funny things start to happen – namely arguments.[1] I suggest setting a timer (your microwave has one) for twenty minutes. If you aren't finished with your Role Play when the alarm sounds, pause the conversation and take a break. Set the timer again when you reconvene.

---

[1] They're funny for the rest of us when they occur in public. Go ahead and try to keep your voices down as you duke it out, we'll pretend we don't hear everything that's going on.

Once the French maid has given his or her feedback and you've come to terms with your budget for the month ahead, the fireman must make any necessary revisions.

You did it! You've got a contract in place for the next month!

Now you can go *play*!

It sounds so easy, doesn't it?

Here are a few principles by which to run your Role Play so that you both stay on track in unity:

First, firemen have a tendency to be very protective of their budget. They generally enjoy taking the time to put it together and the idea that a French maid is going to critique it can be very frustrating. Firemen, do not allow defensiveness to creep into the Role Play. Serve your French maids by hearing them out.

Second, French maids have a tendency of finding other life activities more exciting than the Role Play – okay, basically *any* other life activity. French maids, you must come to the Role Play and contribute to the process. Carving out this time to build a regular, productive financial dialogue can literally divorce-proof your marriage. It's serious business, but you can certainly have fun with it.

Third, commit to holding each other accountable. Have your goals lying right there on the table when you're discussing next month's budget. Are you making decisions that propel you closer to or drag you farther from what you desire to accomplish together? Don't be afraid to remind each other – in love, of course – how great it will be to reach those goals as husband and wife, French maid and fireman. In practice, if any expenses arise outside of what you planned in your budget, you must talk it over together before any money is paid.

Role Plays are opportunities to cultivate trust and foster

communication. Don't let your spouse down by not pulling your weight or playing your role.

budgeting in the buff

Budgets scare people.

I recently met with a client who rescheduled our first session together four times because he was afraid I was going to tell him he couldn't spend any money.[1]

That's what a lot of people equate with a budget. "Budget" equals "You can't spend money or enjoy anything. How's your tuna fish sandwich?"

In truth, creating a monthly budget (call it a spending plan if it makes you and your spouse feel better) is the only way you'll adequately account for your regular monthly expenses *and* work toward accomplishing your short- and long-term goals.

John Maxwell says, "A budget is telling your money where to go rather than wondering where it went." According to Maxwell, a budget is how you control money that flows through your household, not how to prevent yourself from having a life.

What I like most about putting together a monthly budget with Elisa is the conversation we get to have. Knowing that we're both financially united month in and month out has power. It's one less thing we have to stress about.

According to a *Wall Street Journal* study, nearly 70% of Americans live paycheck-to-paycheck. I'm convinced a lot of those people are living that type of existence because they "manage" their money by facing backwards.

---

[1] Coincidentally, this very same client paid cash for a home two months earlier.

Alright, let's call it what it really is: they aren't "managing" anything; they're simply tracking where the money already went.

This is a *reactive* method. We see the money come in, we react with jubilee, we see the money go out, we react with horror because there's too much month at the end of the money.[1] There are plenty of great tools out there on the market that you can use to track your spending, from Quicken to Mint.com.[2] However, simply watching how money is spent doesn't make you an effective money manager.

You're looking for the *proactive* method of budgeting. We've already talked about the Role Play occurring *before* each month begins. The reasoning is simple: no two months are ever the same. Sure, there are plenty of generally static expenses (mortgage or rent, insurance, giving, and utilities), but you don't have Christmas each month.

Nor do you have summer vacations each month.

And you won't be buying more decorative pillows for your bed each month.[3]

With your roles clearly defined, it's time to create this budget for you and your spouse so you're both moving into the coming month *together*. Robert Wolgemuth puts it like this: "The beauty of accountability *to a budget* is that, at least in some sense, when you allow your budget to determine your spending decisions, you avoid being pitted against each other. In effect, you let the budget be the referee."[4]

Use this next worksheet to plan *next month's* expenses you and your

---

[1] You'll hear some folks call this Thank-God-it's-Friday-Oh-God-it's-Monday Syndrome.
[2] I don't use either of these; just Excel for this fireman.
[3] I suggest downsizing to a queen bed to limit this type of activity; plus you'll cuddle more, which helps save on the heating bill.
[4] The Most Important Year in a Man's Life, page 101.

spouse will incur. Schedule your Role Play to finalize your proactive budget and then honor each other by staying accountable.

our naked monthly budget (spending plan)

Spending Category	Planned Amount	Non-Monthly Expense	Actual Amount
Giving			
Savings			
Emergency Savings			
Other Savings			
IRA Contributions			
Self-employment Taxes			
Housing			
First Mortgage/Rent			
Second Mortgage			
Home Repairs/Maintenance			
Homeowner/Renter Insurance			
Real Estate Taxes			
Homeowner's Association			
Pest Control/Lawn Care			
Utilities			
Electricity			
Water			
Gas			
Cable/Phone/Internet			
Trash/Sewer			
Mobile Phone			
Security System			
Food			
Groceries			
Eating Out			

Transportation				
Car Payment 1				
Car Payment 2				
Other Vehicle Payment(s)				
Fuel				
Repairs/Oil/Tires				
Auto Insurance				
Registration/Inspection				
AAA/Roadside Assistance				
Personal Needs				
Clothing				
Personal Care/Hair Care				
Other Insurance				
Disability Insurance				
Health Insurance				
Long-term Care Insurance				
Life Insurance				
Prescriptions/Co-pays				
Other Spending				
Birthday/Wedding Gifts				
Christmas Gifts				
Childcare/Tuition				
Entertainment				
Vacation/Travel				
Walkin' Around Money				
Subscriptions				
Memberships				
Peace, Love & Harmony				
Other:				
Other:				
Other:				
TOTAL				

Even though I've provided you with a template to help you create your budget together, you're more than welcome to change it. Go ahead! Add categories, change names, do whatever you need to do in order to make your monthly budget your own.

As for the rest of the His and Hers worksheets, it's time you converted those to Ours, too!

our naked income sources

Source	Monthly Amount	Pay Frequency
Salary 1		
Salary 2		
Salary 3		
Self-employment		
Bonuses		
Child Support		
Investments (Interest, Dividends, etc.)		
Disability		
Social Security		
Unemployment		
Other:		
TOTAL:		

Be sure to identify who is bringing each stream of income to the table in the worksheet above.

our naked consumer debt

Debt Type	Outstanding Balance	Minimum Payment	Interest Rate
Credit Cards			
Retail Loans			
Vehicle Loans			
Personal Loans			
Student Loans			
TOTAL			

Use an asterisk to indicate on the worksheet above if any of the debts are past due.

our naked net worth

Item	Asset	Liability	Equity
1st Mortgage			
2nd Mortgage			
Vehicle 1			
Vehicle 2			
Vehicle 3			
Cash On Hand			
Checking Account 1			
Checking Account 2			
Checking Account 3			
Savings Account 1			
Savings Account 2			
Savings Account 3			
Money Market Account			
Brokerage Account			
Retirement Plan 1			
Retirement Plan 2			
Retirement Plan 3			
Stocks & Bonds			
Antiques & Collectibles			
Boats & Other Vehicles			
Unsecured Debt (negative)			
IRS Debt (negative)			
Other:			
Other:			
TOTAL			

So, how does it all look? With both of your worlds combined, does it feel like you're getting naked?

With goals in place, a complete record of your financial position as a couple, and an understanding of what you must do every month to manage your resources wisely, let's now turn our gaze to the initial targets you must aim toward.

the naked truth

Ethan is an accountant. His wife Anna is a professional, too. They had been married for about a year when we first sat down to create a savings and debt elimination strategy. About fifteen minutes into our conversation Anna revealed that she felt like there was a huge gulf between her and Ethan over money matters. She explained that every month they would write checks back and forth to each other to pay utility bills and the mortgage.

When I suggested that the gulf would never go away, that they wouldn't experience complete financial or relational unity until they combined bank accounts, and that separate is inherently unequal, you could've heard a pin drop.

Ethan is a professional money manager, but his skills and experience were working against him at home. Anna didn't need a CPA; she needed a husband who was willing to welcome her input. After their first meeting with me they opened joint checking and savings accounts.

When we met a month later they were both smiling and giddy. Anna said she couldn't remember ever talking with Ethan so much about money and what would be best for them as a couple. For Ethan, he said that combining their financial worlds challenged him to stop handling money like a bachelor and honor the woman he married.

As a word of caution to men – particularly men who are firemen – beware the opportunities to steamroll your wife during financial discussions. "There are few places where husbands make more mistakes than when they're dealing with money. Here's a good rule to remember: if you speak to your wife about money as though she were a child, then she will believe that your concern over money is more important than your love for her."[1]

Now that you've come together...

let's get it on!

I can't overstate the importance of this section of the book. Experience has shown me time and again that with a little bit of prodding, normal, everyday people are capable of accomplishing extraordinary, remarkable feats.

The goals you've set for the months and years ahead will help you stay focused on what matters most to you both. As you kick-start your life in financial unity, I'm going to challenge you with some initial targets that simply can't be disregarded.

From intentionally scheduling time to talk about money (without other interruptions), to putting together an emergency fund *fast*, to systematically dumping any outstanding consumer debt, my desire is for you both to experience intimacy, peace, and downright passion about crossing the finish line of a financial goal together.

pick you up around 7:00?

Don't get confused, *I'm* not asking you out.

What you absolutely must do is commit to a date and time each month that you will have your Role Play. Firemen shouldn't expect French maids to have an attention span much longer than the twenty minutes you'll put on the timer. French maids shouldn't expect the firemen to prepare the budget and pass along a Cliffs Notes version.

---

[1] The Most Important Year in a Man's Life, page 102. We could easily rewrite this paragraph for the lady firemen out there who berate their husbands with the monthly budget. Either way, it's bad news for your relationship and your money.

We live in a day and age where distractions lurk around every corner and it can be very easy to push discussions about money to the burner behind the burner behind the back burner. Just last week, a couple I'm working with pulled out their Blackberries and scheduled a date for a Sunday afternoon at the end of the month to talk about the coming month's budget.

They picked a time when their kids take naps.

M. Scott Peck says, "You cannot truly listen and do anything else at the same time." Even if you don't have young children, you'll need to shut off whatever sporting event or Food Network show might be on and devote your full, undivided attention to your spouse.

Here's my promise: if you'll commit to your Role Play for six months, you'll find that you won't spend more than ten minutes a month formally discussing your financial strategy and budget.

How do I know this? Elisa and I spend five minutes a month reviewing the previous and coming months. Since we've developed a running, open dialogue about money over the years, I come to our Role Play with a spending plan that's about 95% complete for the month ahead. We also know that we accomplish our goals if we live according to our spending plan and that we'll get to add a new goal each time one is checked off.[1]

So, make it a date. You won't be managing your money together like you truly desire in twelve months if you give up on the Role Play after three months.

reality bites

Since few of the people I meet with have created a legitimate forward-looking budget, let's take the time to establish two feet grounded firmly in reality. Some of us are a little disconnected in our understanding of what things *actually* cost.

---

[1] Notice how I call it a "spending plan"? That gives Elisa a warm fuzzy.

And this is coming from a guy who used to live on $80 a month for groceries!

When planning your monthly expenses, always err on the high side. This will give you a conservative perspective on the cash flow requirements of next month's income. Aside from not stressing out as much as you would with a rigid budget (that goes bust one week into the month when you overspend your scrapbooking category by $2.00), you'll get the added benefit of flexibility should an unexpected expense arise. Reallocating funds between categories within the budget will prevent needless dips into the emergency fund.

In planning a flexible budget, there are two categories you must pay very close attention to: groceries and eating out. Hands down, these are the two biggest budget busters for the vast majority of couples. I once met with a couple who spent $200 a month on groceries and $600 a month eating out. There's nothing wrong with going out to eat, but food expenses as a whole consumed a quarter of their take-home pay.[1]

When planning your grocery budget, a good baseline is estimating about $150-$175 per person per month in the household. This includes both food and basic toiletry needs for each person, by the way. As for eating out, understand that you will generally pay four to six times more for a meal in a restaurant compared to a meal at home.[2]

The flipside of the Reality Bites coin is that you're also going to have to say "No" when you're budgeting.[3] In terms of spending, recognize that any dollar you spend on one category is a dollar less to spend on any other category.[4] As you look at how you and your

---

[1] They were literally eating themselves out of house and home! [Insert rim shot here.]
[2] You should read Sex Begins in the Kitchen by Dr. Kevin Leman; cheaper than eating out and much better dessert.
[3] I'm not a fan of just saying "No". If you say "No" to anything, identify what you'll say "Yes" to in the long run.
[4] This is what economics buffs call "opportunity cost."

spouse allocate money among the different spending categories, understand that you will be incorporating your short- and long-term goals into your budget at the same time.

Thus, for every dollar you allocate to groceries, that's one dollar less to allocate to savings.

And for every dollar you allocate to savings, that's one dollar less to allocate to entertainment.

And for every dollar you allocate to entertainment, that's one dollar less to allocate to debt.

With grace and love, remember that you'll have to work together to control spending in order to accomplish what you desire as a couple.

risky business

When I say the words "financial emergency," what comes to mind?

The transmission goes on your vehicle?

The hot water heater dies mid-shampoo rinse?

You make a visit to the ER?

You lose your job?

We could list all sorts of scary, unexpected, expensive trials with the potential to wreak havoc on your household economy. Studies even show that it's not a matter of *if* a financial emergency occurs, but *when* it will occur.

Money magazine reports that 78% of Americans will face a substantial, negative financial event in any given ten-year period. Meanwhile, "in the house of the wise are stores of choice food and oils, but a foolish man devours all he has."[1] Life is risky business and smart people mitigate that risk with cash savings.

The initial target range for a good starter emergency fund is $1,000 – $1,500. Put this money in a plain-Jane savings or money market account. Remember, this is not considered an investment because you may need it tomorrow and exposing it to the volatility of the stock market is bad risk management.

I wish I could catch on camera when my clients tell me they've established their first emergency fund. I've worked with a few people who've never had more than $200 in the bank, let alone $1,000. The peace that washes over their faces is captivating.

To experience this peace you'll need to get radical! If you can't establish an emergency fund right away, you need to use your budget to create as much additional monthly savings as possible. Likewise, look around the newlywed pad – I'm sure you can find sellable items you won't ever use again.[2] Use that money to fill out your emergency fund, as well.

Aside from experiencing peace and stability, having emergency savings is actually the first step out of consumer debt. Without a cash safety net, you'd have to put an unexpected expense on a credit card or use other borrowed funds. That perpetuates the consumer debt cycle. With savings in place, you pay for the expense and move on; you won't have to relive it in the form of interest and payments.

shed the debt

The Bible compares indebtedness to slavery: "The rich rule over the poor and the borrower is slave to the lender."[3]

---

1 Proverbs 21:20.
2 Oh please! I got married once, too; I know you have stuff you aren't using at all.
3 Proverbs 22:7.

If you haven't had the light bulb moment yet, recognize that if you have consumer debt payments in your life, you work for a master.

Seriously. A portion of your workday is for someone else when you have a bill to pay.[1]

Here's some math for you:

If you make $50,000 a year, you're earning about $24 per hour ($50,000 ÷ 52 weeks/year ÷ 40 hours/week). Let's say you have monthly debt payments of $600 (a car loan, student loan, and credit card payment).

That's $7,200 per year, right?

In order to make your payments, you go to work and earn your $24 each hour. But your monthly debt is costing you $3.46 per hour ($7,200 ÷ 52 weeks/year ÷ 40 hours/week).

Wait, you don't actually *realize* $24 per hour, do you? Of course not! Ol' Uncle Sam has a hand in the cookie jar. If you take out 20% of your pay for taxes, you really get home with $19.23 per hour.[2]

Okay, let's flip the switch and turn that light bulb on!

If you divide the cost of your debt by your take-home pay, you can see what portion of each hour of work is devoted to repaying your consumer debt. $3.46 divided by $19.23 equals 18%.

18% of each hour you work – or about 11 minutes – is not for you. It's for your creditors.

Every hour.

---
1 If the light bulb still isn't on, keep reading.
2 I know you're thinking, "Please Derek! Enough with the arithmetic! I bought this book to learn how to make lots of money and have lots of sex with my spouse!" Bear with me just a few short moments longer...

Every workday.

Illuminating, isn't it?

In my math example above, I used $600 a month for debt payments. Do you know that if you invest that each month from the time you're married until your 25th wedding anniversary, you'll have about $800,000 on hand?[1]

I'm a huge fan of the debt snowball approach to dumping debt for good. With your consumer debt worksheet handy, rearrange your debts from smallest balance to largest balance. Pay the minimum amounts on each debt except for the smallest – attack that one with a vengeance!

Find as much extra cash flow in your budget as possible and consider selling more stuff to pay extra on that debt until it disappears. Once it's gone, you can roll all that additional cash flow plus the previous minimum payment into the next debt. Each time you do this your payments will grow (like a snowball, how witty!) until you unleash an avalanche on your largest debts.

Generally, the debt snowball is a great approach for helping you stay motivated and enthusiastic about shedding your debt with your spouse. By paying off smaller balances first, you'll get a quick sense of accomplishment that will propel you forward.

Remember the story I told about Mark and Natalie? They were so enamored with having the same (or better) lifestyle as their parents that they had to borrow to fund it. Don't fall into that trap and waste the time your money could be earning interest by paying someone else interest.

Aside from the math working against you, there is a tremendous weight on a newly married couple under the burden of debt.

---

[1] For the finance geeks, if you do this until your 50th anniversary you'll have over $10 million and will be able to get the best hearing aids and hip replacements money can buy!

Creditors are like uninvited guests who don't go home. They just stay in the guestroom wanting you to wait on them all the time.[1]

the most wonderful time of the year[2]

Newsflash: Christmas is in December this year.

What?! You've got to be kidding me!

No joke – December 25th – and the second best time to start saving is *right now*![3]

Unfortunately, many of us stumble into the holidays. It's as if we get three Augusts in a row and then – *bam!* – it's November. Without preparing for the presents, travel, and food of the holidays, most couples rely on credit cards to pay their way from Black Friday to New Year's.

And by the third week of January, we get a statement of damages.

Aside from Christmas, there will be other non-monthly expenses that you'll plan for like insurance premiums, vehicle repairs, property taxes, membership dues, ad nauseum. We already talked about incorporating them into your monthly budget. Now you'll need to move those dollars to a special holding place until they're ready to be used.

Just like with the emergency fund, I recommend having a separate savings account for holding these non-monthly expenses. You'll put a portion of money for each of those categories in the account each month until it's time to write a check or use some cash for the expense. This will keep a nice tidy boundary line between your

---

1   If you don't have a guestroom, it's like that friend that's sleeping on your couch just until they "get on their feet," only you know they probably won't.
2   Turns out, it's not the NCAA Basketball Tournament.
3   Actually, the best time to begin saving for Christmas is in January – gives you 12 months to spread out your savings plan.

checking account and these short-term savings.

Another great category to lump in with non-monthly expenses is vacation travel. If you plan a few trips throughout the year, simply total up what you anticipate spending and divide by twelve. That figure is what you should set aside each month to accommodate travel expenses. Now you won't have to come up with $500 in November's budget alone to buy airplane tickets to see Aunt Mabel for Thanksgiving.[1]

walkin' around money[2]

I spent a lot of time emphasizing the need to combine your financial world with your spouse's. Your unity, intimacy, and true oneness hung in the balance. Now I'm going to tell you to spend money separately – no questions asked – because it's good for your relationship.

A line item in your monthly budget should be blow money, fun money, or walkin' around money. Each month you and your spouse will have an equal amount to spend or save however you see fit. Since it's written on the budget, you can live like it's already spent. This is a judgment-free category, you see, so don't get critical if your husband spends his on power tools he'll never use, nor if your wife spends hers on smelly candles for each room of your home.

In order to build some controls around this, use actual green cash for your walkin' around money. This way, once it's gone, it's gone – there's no opportunity to overspend what is allotted.

Some couples I know even create a supplemental category for their walkin' around money called *Peace, Love & Harmony*, and include it as a line item on their budget. They might throw $25 – $50 in there each month just in case something comes up and they need the wiggle room. We call it *Peace, Love & Harmony* because that is

---

[1] She gave you that China set and she'll be glad to guilt-trip you into coming.
[2] My Grandpa Sisterhen always says a person should have a little bit of this in their pocket.

what you preserve by having those dollars available.

What if the guys invite your man out to the latest testosterone-soaked action movie, but the entertainment budget is tapped out?

What if your girl is invited to a jewelry or housewares "party" by a bunch of her friends, but she's out of walkin' around money?[1]

A little flexibility with a *Peace, Love & Harmony* category can help pad your walkin' around money and disarm a lot of argument bombs. Again, this whole concept of walkin' around money is specifically designed to give each of you some individuality in the budget, so enjoy.

And maybe buy your honey something nice with it every once in a while.

the naked truth

When Derek and Elisa were married, Derek had about $16,000 outstanding on a car loan...

That's right: the first thing I did after graduating from college was go out and buy a snazzy, brand new, four-door car because I wanted to "look like a professional."[2]

Since I'm a "smart" finance guy, I knew enough to put a hefty down payment on the car so I'd never be upside-down. What I got was a sweet new ride, monthly payments of $410, and monthly depreciation averaging $400. That's right, "smart" finance guy was

---

[1] A Derek Soapbox Moment: Nothing like a gathering of folks guilt-tripped into making purchases they otherwise wouldn't – purchases that will likely wind up in a yard sale pile within two years – all to support a friend/co-worker/relative. Men, you'll learn to stop asking many questions about these things like I did.

[2] My paid-for pickup truck didn't feel adequate any longer. Ironically, I'd give the guy who bought it his money back if I could have it again. I loved that truck... I called her 'Ol Bess...she was awesome...

losing over $800 in total value each month.

I brought the loan into my marriage. When Elisa and I compared our *Dreams & Goals* worksheets, we both agreed it was time to dump the car loan. I ran some numbers to find out how long it would take to pay off the balance if we really buckled down. I told Elisa that if we cut out all of the fun, all of the fluff, and all the wiggle room in our budget, we could have the car loan completely paid off in four months.

I thought for sure that she would say, "Run the numbers again – this time so we can *have a life*! It's your loan, by the way!"

Instead, she said, "I know it's going to be a rough four months, but we have to be debt-free."[1]

Beginning in the month of December, we turned our thermostat down to 60 degrees. We didn't go out to eat. We didn't take any trips.

We only used cash to buy groceries.

Our only luxury was basic cable. (I justified it because the TV put off some heat and warmed the room a little bit when it was on.)

We lived on less than my paycheck. Any money leftover was added to Elisa's paycheck and sent to the bank each month.

In March of that following year – a mere four months after we started – the couple that was hanging by a thread over $40 worth of pillows a few months earlier paid off a $16,000 car loan.

And we did it together.

Today, Elisa and I look back on that period of time and laugh. We laugh at how we'd have no less than five blankets piled on our bed

---
1   To this day, I'm still very grateful for the sacrifices she made so we could accomplish that goal together.

to stay warm. We laugh at how we'd huddle together on the couch to share body heat while watching *Survivor* on TV. We laugh at how much cereal we ate for dinner. We laugh at how long we went without leaving the town we lived in.

We laugh.

And I don't even care that, because of the sacrifices I asked Elisa to make with me, I'm going to drive my car until the wheels fall off. You don't really care what you're driving when you're debt-free and experiencing financial intimacy with your spouse.

After getting naked financially and cultivating an atmosphere of intimacy in your financial conversations, we can now turn our attention to the two of you staying naked in your marriage.

chapter seven

"The man and his wife were both naked, and they felt no shame."

-Genesis 2:25

the big picture

When we step back and view the financial forest for the trees, we see a lot more going on than two people filling out budget spreadsheets each month.

Earlier we talked about real love being a choice rather than a feeling. The root of that choice is respect. "Respect says, 'I support you, you are valuable to me, and you don't have to be any different from who you are.'"[1] We could probably say that you have to respect a person before you can get naked with them in an authentic way.

In truth, your legacy as husband and wife begins the moment you say *I do*. You'll hear older folks drop that word – *legacy* – because they want their mark on the world to last longer than they do.

---

1 Saving Your Marriage Before it Starts, page 104.

When you think about it, though, everyone leaves a legacy. There will always be *something* future generations remember you by.

In the big picture, with a foundation of respect for your marriage and a commitment to financial unity, your children will have proper role models creating a positive, lasting legacy.

the givers gain

I'm going to let you in on a little secret that you may not be aware of.

You don't own anything.

We've spent the last six chapters talking about how to manage all these different resources you have in your possession and I'm just now telling you that you don't own any of it.

Psalm 24:1 says, "The earth is the Lord's, and everything in it, the world, and all who live in it."[1] So, that means that all the money and all the stuff in your keeping – including your plaid-upholstered recliner – belongs to Him.

We're called *stewards*, which means we have no ownership over anything, but are entrusted to manage the resources we've been given as effectively as possible. And yet, we're told that the best use of these resources is to bless others around us. Paul writes in Acts, "We must help the weak, remembering the words the Lord Jesus himself said: 'It is more blessed to give than to receive.'"[2]

I love how *The Message* phrases this verse: "You're far happier giving than receiving."

I have yet to find one person who will answer "Yes" when I ask, "Do you want to give less money and help fewer people?" We all know of needs in our community and people who are struggling.

---
1   Go take a peek at Psalm 24 in its entirety if you haven't recently.
2   Acts 20:35.

By following through with what we've discussed in this book, you'll be able to save tremendous amounts of money and build wealth. How much fun could you have as a couple giving a portion of that money to others in creative ways?

Tip a waitress $100 and then run out of the restaurant like you're dining and dashing.

Adopt a family in need at Christmas, buy presents and groceries, and play Santa for them.

If you have friends with kids, offer to babysit and give them a gift card to a restaurant they like.[1]

Go on a mission trip together.

Injecting fun and creativity into your giving discipline is Biblical: "Each man should give what he has decided in his heart to give, not reluctantly or under compulsion, for God loves a cheerful giver."[2] Giving cheerfully and creatively is infectious; you'll continue to look for ways to one-up a prior giving spree together.

Though you don't need to bother with who notices your giving discipline, you will capture the attention of the little ones who bear your last name and facial features. This is how a philanthropic legacy spans generations.

the pittering and pattering of little feet

Children present a whole new set of financial challenges to a married couple. First, they cost a fortune.[3]

---

1   Elisa and I did this for some great friends and had an absolute blast; we're hoping our friends had enough fun to get naked that night! [I hope that's not too weird to say.]
2   2 Corinthians 9:7.
3   The U.S. Department of Agriculture reports that it costs between $180,000 and $250,000 to raise a child from birth to age 18.

Second, they will carry on your legacy, so you have to teach them to handle money wisely.

To that second point, it makes sense when we read, "Train a child in the way he should go, and when he is old he will not turn from it." My guess is you probably never realized that this verse is immediately followed with, "The rich rule over the poor and the borrower is slave to the lender."[1]

Interesting stuff: I'm supposed to train my child in wisdom and – oh, by the way, Junior – debt is a ball and chain that will wrap itself around your ankles.

The financial education of children begins at home and you're responsible as parents. When you show your children what a marriage relationship is supposed to look like – that a husband and wife are committed to working through difficult times, that they aren't afraid to show affection, and that they are engaged in productive financial conversation – that becomes their version of *normal*.

They will carry it into their lives as adults and they will carry it into their marriages.[2]

What if your kids see you openly giving as a part of your family's financial plan? You have the opportunity to raise financially balanced kids: they'll give and save money before they spend.

This is how a great marriage spills into multiple generations. You pay it forward when you train your children in the way they should go.

That pittering and pattering sound is created by the same feet that will carry forth your legacy. Who cares if *your* parents never taught you about money? You can change the direction of your family tree by doing right by your kids.

---
1 Proverbs 22:6-7.
2 Re-read "Your Designer Set of Baggage" in Chapter 2 again if you need to.

don't settle for mediocrity

I don't think too many people set out to have mediocre marriages. At least I sure hope not!

All throughout this book, I've been making subtle references to your financial intimacy having a direct and material impact on your physical intimacy.

Consider this my not-so-subtle reference.

Why would anyone want to make love with their spouse when they aren't experiencing financial intimacy?

Now, I know a lot of you who aren't on the same financial page are still having sex – there are little babies to prove it! I'm not a marriage counselor or sex therapist, but my guess is that many married folks are having sex out of obligation rather than a deep desire for passion with their lover.

To make matters worse, I'm afraid that some of these folks wind up thinking that this is simply what the average married couple does. That's not a good place to be, thinking your marriage is average.

From Song of Solomon:

Lover: "How beautiful you are, my darling! Oh, how beautiful! Your eyes are doves."

Beloved: "How handsome you are, my lover! Oh, how charming! And our bed is verdant."

Lover: "The beams of our house are cedars; our rafters are firs."[1]

So...er...um, when was the last time you and your spouse made love outside, in the grass, under the trees?

---

1   Song of Solomon 1:15-17.

It's Biblical, you know.[1]

When you become *one flesh* with your spouse, unite two separate financial worlds, and commit to offer each other grace, mercy, and love for the rest of your lives, you are creating a new paradigm for the Institution of Marriage.

Clearly, we've seen throughout the Bible that this way of doing life in marriage isn't actually *new*, but compared to how your marriage fits into our current culture, this way is revolutionary. This way is everything but mediocre.

I use the scene from Song of Solomon to illustrate the need to avoid conventionality. We already know that 84% of those in conventional marriages deal with major tension and stress in their relationships over money.

So, get outside.

As you commit to and invest further in your marriage, your intimacy and passion will grow. Your communication about money will become second nature; money is just another part of being married.

Like sex.

Like children.

Like giving.

Like serving others.

As husband and wife, you get to experience all life has to offer together. Make this life and marriage count by whatever means necessary – even if you have to go outside – to avoid mediocrity.

---

[1] Men reading this are rejoicing saying, "This is why I bought this book!"

God at the center

My guess is the last wedding you attended included language like, "Therefore what God has joined together, let no man put asunder." You probably heard it at your own wedding if the minister was worth his salt.

This isn't some contrived phrase that man has conjured up to sound spiritually affirming for newlyweds. In fact, the phrase came straight from Jesus' mouth.[1] He was reminding the Pharisees – or religious zealots of the time (still plenty of those around, huh?) – that when a man and woman marry they become *one flesh*, joined by God.

God created marriage before Adam knew what hit him. Adam was just getting the hang of naming all the animals when he pitched in a rib for Eve. After he woke up from the transplant, I can only imagine the very first introduction to the very first eligible bachelorette by an all-powerful Matchmaker.

Adam: "Hey Eve, how you doin'? I named that one over there 'tiger'." [Makes pawing motion.]

Eve: "Is that so?"

God: [Rolls eyes.]

Earlier we talked about marriage being counter-cultural. That marriage is about you becoming less and your spouse becoming more goes directly against the humanistic grain. God created this for His joy and His delight because He loves when we serve one another. We know this because when Jesus walked among us He was the consummate servant.[2]

St. Augustine said, "Thou has made us for Thyself, and our hearts are restless 'til they rest in Thee." We cannot expect ourselves

---

1 Matthew 19:6.
2 John 13:12-17. Get crazy naked, vulnerable, and humble: wash your spouse's feet.

to reach the heights of satisfaction that marriage can provide by keeping God at arm's length. Nor will we realize the profound joy that comes from effectively managing the resources we've received if He's not involved in the discussion.

You can keep God at the center of your marriage by regularly praying together as husband and wife. Make this a discipline because life will come at you fast from time to time and your kneejerk reaction must be to turn to the One who created marriage in the first place.

God's love for you is endless.[1]

God's will is perfect.[2]

God's purpose for your life is exceptionally meaningful.[3]

In prayer we can discern these things together and develop a level of intimacy in our marriages that would be impossible otherwise. And interestingly enough, the spiritual health of your marriage has substantial physical importance. According to *Saving Your Marriage Before it Starts*, "As strange as it may sound, there is a strong link in marriage between prayer and sex."[4]

Not only does the couple that prays together stay together, the couple that prays together also *lays* together![5]

staying naked

The verse from Genesis that opened this chapter comes just before

---

1 Lamentations 3:22-23.
2 Romans 12:2.
3 Jeremiah 29:11.
4 Saving Your Marriage Before it Starts, page 145.
5 And I mean "lay" in a VERY Biblical sense of the word. See also "begat." Also, for the English buffs out there, I recognize correct grammar is to say "lies" in this situation. However, "lies" doesn't rhyme with "prays," so deal with it.

the chronicle of The Fall. All at once, Adam and Eve were coexisting in a world without sin, without pride, without envy, without judgment, without clothes, and they felt no shame.

I'm not so naive to believe that you can have a marriage completely removed from the reality of our fallen world. There will be sin, pride, envy, judgment, and clothes in your marriage relationship. How you wade through those choppy waters says much about your individual character and the resilience of your marriage.

But what if you could recapture just a smidge of what that must have been like so long ago? What if you could be completely exposed – physically, financially, emotionally – and look upon your spouse with such love that he or she wouldn't feel ashamed for a second?

I do believe you can work and strive and persevere and commit with all your might to grasp a sliver of that life. If you allow yourself to be that vulnerable with your lover, elevating his or her needs above your own, and trusting wholeheartedly in the vows you made to each other, I believe you can experience a taste of the peace Adam and Eve had in Eden.

This will only be possible if you constantly, regularly choose to honor your marriage relationship in the eyes of your spouse and of God for the rest of your lives.

Until death do you part.

Sounds awfully heavy.

Sounds awfully fulfilling, too.

You get married to someone you want to *do* life with. This is the person with whom you'll share your existence. To draw them into you at the deepest of all possible levels is to fulfill God's purpose for the Covenant of Marriage.

We know that money will touch every aspect of your marriage, but keep money in its right place. Your marriage matters so much more. Don't forget it.

Even if collectors are calling about past due bills.

Even if you don't get the promotion and you can't buy the dream house.

Even if you wind up with tons of money.

If you do what we've talked about in this book, you'll be financially successful. And yet, I'd strongly advise you not to do these things *just* to be financially successful.

Do them because your marriage – the relationship where a husband and wife are naked before each other and feel no shame – depends on it.

So, here's to staying naked.

stripping down to money and marriage

get naked

afterword

It is a true pleasure to leave you with a few words of encouragement. I am so proud of my husband for writing this book. I know it has the power to be marriage-enhancing – it was for us! So, please be encouraged. It is my prayer that the wisdom in this book has given you the practical resources to transform your marriage and your family tree. It may take time, but there is hope!

After reading some of our stories, I'm sure you can imagine that Derek and I have come a long way in how we relate with money and each other. We can laugh about it all now; it's fun to reflect on our progress. Hint: If you want to be encouraged, look back over the progress you and your spouse make! You gain the motivation to push forward when you can remember past successes.

I can honestly tell you that Derek and I have reached a deeper level of intimacy than I had imagined possible in our years of marriage. This level of intimacy was largely a direct result of getting real with each other financially.

We still have our moments, to be sure, and that's okay. As a scrooge and a free spirit, we are two different people with two different views. But because we are committed to making it work and have learned how to approach each other, we can talk productively and make decisions that honor both of us. Oftentimes, it also involves dying to our selfish tendencies.

My advice to you is this: it may not be easy, but the sooner you get real with your spouse about money, the better. It took me time to realize this truth: it's okay that Derek and I are different. We just have to come up with a solution that works best for the both of us; it's no longer just about me anymore. You may have to do the same reality check. Identify your strengths and weaknesses, your personality types, your shared dreams and goals. It will be revolutionary!

Derek knows what he is talking about. Every nugget of wisdom in this book can and will change your life. He and I are living proof of its success. I am awed by his heart and his ability to share such wisdom with you, so that you, too, can experience deep intimacy with your spouse in all areas of life.

So, get naked! It's the best thing you will ever do!

I wish you well,

Elisa Sisterhen

stripping down to money and marriage

get naked

appendices

appendix 1: sample naked worksheets

To help you see how to lay out your own *Naked Worksheets*, I went ahead a put together some samples for you.

our naked income sources

Source	Monthly Amount	Pay Frequency
Salary 1 – Hers	$2,850	Monthly
Salary 2 – His	$2,570	Bi-weekly ($1,285 per check)
Salary 3		
Self-employment		
Bonuses – His	$150	$450 paid Quarterly
Child Support		
Investments (Interest, Dividends, etc.)		
Disability		
Social Security		
Unemployment		
Other: Commissions – Hers	$200	Monthly
TOTAL:	**$5,770**	

our naked monthly budget (spending plan)

Spending Category	Planned Amount	Non-Monthly Expense	Actual Amount
Giving	$577		
Savings			
Emergency Savings			
Other Savings			

IRA Contributions				
Self-employment Taxes				
Housing				
First Mortgage/Rent	$1,500			
Second Mortgage				
Home Repairs/Maintenance	$75	$75		
Homeowner/Renter Insurance				
Real Estate Taxes				
Homeowner's Association	$80			
Pest Control/Lawn Care	$40			
Utilities				
Electricity	$160			
Water	$60			
Gas	$50			
Cable/Phone/Internet	$125			
Trash/Sewer				
Mobile Phone	$85			
Security System				
Food				
Groceries	$500			
Eating Out	$150			
Transportation				
Car Payment 1	$325			
Car Payment 2				
Other Vehicle Payment(s)				
Fuel	$250			
Repairs/Oil/Tires	$50	$50		
Auto Insurance	$70	$70		
Registration/Inspection				
AAA/Roadside Assistance				
Personal Needs				
Clothing	$50			

Personal Care/Hair Care	$50		
Other Insurance			
Disability Insurance	Employer pays		
Health Insurance	Employer pays		
Long-term Care Insurance			
Life Insurance	Employer pays		
Prescriptions/Co-pays			
Other Spending			
Birthday/Wedding Gifts	$50		
Christmas Gifts	$75	$75	
Childcare/Tuition			
Entertainment	$50		
Vacation/Travel	$125	$125	
Walkin' Around Money	$100		
Subscriptions			
Memberships – Gym	$35		
Peace, Love & Harmony	$50		
Consumer Debt[1]	$520		
Other:			
Other:			
TOTAL	$5,202	$395[2]	

---

1 The Consumer Debt figure doesn't include the Jeep payment. Since that loan is secured by the vehicle, it gets its very own line on the Naked Spending Plan – "Car Payment 1."

2 Taking all the non-monthly expenses and setting them to a monthly schedule means that you'll put $395 into your non-monthly expense savings account. When it's time to take the vacation, pay the insurance premiums, buy some paint for the house, or get an oil change, you'll simply transfer the money back to your checking account to pay for the expense.

our naked consumer debt

Debt Type	Outstanding Balance	Minimum Payment	Interest Rate
Credit Cards			
Visa ending 0123	$2,300	$70	8.99%
Discover ending 0456	$3,500	$105	11.99%
Retail Loans			
Best Buy – TV/DVDs	$1,200	$50	18.25%
Vehicle Loans			
2003 Jeep Wrangler	$7,500	$325	6.50%
Personal Loans			
Cousin Charlie	PAID OFF!!	PAID OFF!!	PAID OFF!!
Student Loans			
Sallie Mae – His	$9,800	$120	4.50%
Sallie Mae – Hers	$11,200	$175	3.75%
TOTAL	$35,500	$845	

stripping down to money and marriage

our naked net worth

Item	Asset	Liability	Equity
1st Mortgage – 20yr fixed @ 6%	$185,000	$148,000	$37,000
2nd Mortgage			
Vehicle 1 – 2003 Jeep Wrangler	$8,000	$7,500	$500
Vehicle 2 – 1998 Chevy S-10	$4,500		$4,500
Vehicle 3			
Cash On Hand	$325		$325
Checking Account 1	$800		$800
Checking Account 2			
Checking Account 3			
Savings Account 1 – Emergency Fund	$1,500		$1,500
Savings Account 2 – Non-monthly Exp	$400		$400
Savings Account 3			
Money Market Account	$500		$500
Brokerage Account			
Retirement Plan 1 – Hers – 401(k)	$3,400		$3,400
Retirement Plan 2 – His – Roth IRA	$5,200		$5,200
Retirement Plan 3			
Stocks & Bonds			
Antiques & Collectibles – China	$1,250		$1,250
Boats & Other Vehicles			
Unsecured Debt (negative)		$28,000	-$28,000[1]
IRS Debt (negative)			
Other: Plaid-upholstered Recliner	$8[2]		$8
Other:			
TOTAL	**$210,883**	**$183,500**	**$27,383**

1 The Unsecured Debt figure excludes the portion of the Jeep loan from the Naked Consumer Debt total.
2 Who knows, maybe someone would pay you $8 for it...

appendix 2: we want to buy a house!

You're married and it's awesome!

You know what would make it better?

Buying a house!

Of course! God bless *our* new home!

Probably one of the biggest financial blunders a newly married couple will make as husband and wife is buying a house before they're ready.

But what does "ready" actually mean?

First, let's understand that buying a house is just as much emotional as it is financial. For the ladies, in particular, there is a desire to nest.[1] For men, they finally get to be "weekend warriors," making the house into that castle they always wanted.

Believe me; I know how much fun it can be to buy a new garden hose and bag of fertilizer.

So, these emotions are at play; realtors call the condition "house fever."

From a financial standpoint, I have relatively regimented criteria for buying a house.

Debt. Your consumer debt should be completely gone before you entertain buying a house. Debt equals risk and having no other payments except a mortgage puts you in a very strong position should a job loss, illness, or other financial emergency befall you. Plus, if you've taken the time to dump your consumer debt, your discipline is likely strong enough to keep you from going back into

---
1 "Nesting" is that word used to justify excessive furniture and curtain purchases.

debt once you move into the new place.

Savings. Before you begin saving for a down payment, you'll first need to save a robust emergency fund. A funny thing happens when you buy a house: you become the landlord.

Water heater problems? That's your problem.

Air conditioning stops working in the middle of summer? What are you going to do about it, boss?

Neighborhood baseball game lands a homerun ball through a window?

You get the idea.

Having a solid emergency fund in place of at least three months' worth of your new monthly expenses is critical to being prepared for the home purchase.

Savings (again). Thanks to changes in lending standards, it is very difficult to get loans for 100% of the purchase price of a house. That doesn't bother me, because I think you're best served saving at least 20% of the purchase price for a down payment.[1]

There are two benefits of going into a mortgage with 20% down. First, you'll avoid Private Mortgage Insurance (PMI). PMI is what mortgage companies use if a borrower defaults on the monthly mortgage payments, but they allow *you* the privilege of paying the premiums. This can cost anywhere from $60 to $80 per month for each $100,000 you borrow to buy the home. So, if you borrow $200,000, you could be paying $160 each month in PMI. That's $1,920 a year for the math nerds ($1,920 you never get back).

Second, when you put 20% down, you have a solid equity position. It took an economic downturn to remind us that real estate values

---

[1] This is in addition to the emergency fund, not including.

don't always go up.[1] If values plateau or decline in your area, you don't have to worry about getting caught owing more on your house than it's worth. If you ever have to get out of a house quickly you want this flexibility on pricing.

The right mortgage. Fortunately, a lot of the garbage mortgages have been filtered out of the market. Still, there will always be someone offering a piece-of-junk loan to folks who don't know better.

Avoid adjustable rate mortgages and go with a fixed rate. You need to know what you're getting yourself into for the life of the loan. Aim for a 15 or 20-year term on your fixed rate mortgage. If you borrowed $200,000 at 6% for 20 years, you'd repay $343,887; if you borrowed for 30 years, you'd repay $431,676.

That's almost $90,000 more in interest! (You can buy a lot of visual stimulation with that.)

Your mortgage payment – including monthly escrow for homeowner's insurance and property taxes – should be no more than 30% of your *take-home* pay. This will allow you to have a life![2] Mortgage lenders will offer you payments of up to 33% of your *gross pay*, but then again their job is to sell money!

If you take this approach when buying your first home together, it will stay the Great American Dream instead of becoming a Great American Nightmare.

But wait, Derek! Are you saying that we should start out renting? Isn't that a huge waste of money?!

One of the pervasive financial myths out there is that renting is a waste of money. I don't believe renting is an ideal, long-term strategy for your residential investment. However, I do believe it

---

1   Real estate is still a great investment that fluctuates about an ever increasing mean. In English, real estate values go up more than they go down.
2   Remember the story of Mark and Natalie.

can be quite effective in helping you make the transition from *I do* to actually owning your own place.

If you determine to get on the same page financially, dump your debt, and save up for a house while you're renting, then renting serves a very noble purpose. It is an intentional short-term stepping stone on the way to one of your financial goals.

Besides, if you can learn to get naked in a rental together, you'll easily be able to get naked in a house when the time comes.

appendix 3: the borrower is slave to the lender-in-law

The shapes and sizes of loans from parents are vast, from a few hundred dollars to help secure the newlywed's first apartment to a down payment on a house.

On paper, borrowing money from parents or other family members seems like a fine idea. They usually don't charge interest (if they do, it's very low) and they don't typically have strict repayment terms.

"Just pay us what you can when you can."

I don't like it at all.

Revisiting Proverbs 22:7, "the borrower is slave to the lender," helps put some things into perspective.

The verse doesn't say, "the borrower pays interest to the lender." This isn't just a simple business transaction when people borrow money – whether from family or a bank. No, this says that the relationship is that of master and servant when money is loaned.

One of the fastest ways to strain a relationship with in-laws is to borrow money from them. Now, here's what is interesting: they won't think anything of it. You and your spouse are their kids and they want to help you.[1]

Yet, of the pressures newlyweds feel (whether real or self-imposed), probably one of the biggest is the need to show the in-laws that you actually are the right person for their child to spend his or her life with. Adding a financial element to that pressure will only compound these feelings.

I met a young woman a couple of years ago who wanted some advice about the money her husband borrowed from his parents right before they were married. She said that she really wanted to

---

[1] Well, your spouse is their kid and you just happen to reap some benefits-by-association in the deal.

pay off the loan, but that he wasn't feeling a pressing burden to do so.

"Every time they come to our apartment, I feel like they're looking to see if we've made any new purchases. And if they see the new centerpiece on our table are they thinking, 'Why are they buying things like that when they owe us money?'" she said to me, clearly frustrated and recalling a recent experience.

"Building a strong, unencumbered relationship with your [in-laws] is an important – and sometimes challenging – goal to set. And your [spouse] wants the same with your parents."[1] I can think of no more stressful form of encumbering than owing money to in-laws. It will change the way you relate to them until the debt is paid in full.

I told the woman that she and her husband needed to talk seriously about the loan. She needed to explain her position on the matter and remind him that they are one flesh now. I wish he was with her when we spoke; I would've told him to serve his wife on this one and start paying off the debt.

Let's put the shoe on the other foot. Remember in Chapter 3 when we discussed how men have a deeply rooted desire to provide for their wives? What happens to the psyche of a husband who loses his job, but still has a loan from his in-laws to repay? Not only is the ability to provide coming under fire, but also the demonstration to his wife's parents that he can take care of their little girl *and* take responsibility for his debt.

Even if they say, "Pay what you can when you can," we all know that this husband is going to feel incredibly burdened emotionally.

Borrowing money from family changes your relationship with them and spills into your marriage.

Besides, who wants to eat Christmas dinner with their master-in-law?

---

1   The Most Important Year in a Man's Life, page 104.

appendix 4: what about abuse?

I never really knew just how devastating financial infidelity could be until I began working with couples and individuals as their financial coach.

I witnessed one young marriage unravel rapidly after a spouse revealed a hidden stash of credit cards that held tens of thousands of dollars in debt. The other spouse went from believing that she and her husband were just starting to experience life together to the brink of bankruptcy in a matter of moments.

Good friend and Christian marriage counselor April Miller says that financial infidelity is not unlike sexual infidelity. The desire to do something in secret does not cultivate intimacy nor cultivate *one flesh*. The loss of trust in a marriage puts the relationship on a collision course with divorce. However, with willing hearts and help, couples in these situations can reconcile and get back to a satisfying life together.

First, when uncovering the abuse determine whether counseling is needed. That may be a difficult determination to make if you're caught up in the emotional roller coaster ride. If the abuse is over $1,000 in total secretive spending, I believe counseling is a must.

Ultimately, what must be understood is why the spouse is spending without being honest. Whether a wife is spending here and there saying, "He'll never find out," or a husband is racking up thousands of dollars in expenses, there are reasons for this lack of openness in the marriage and a counselor can help unpack them.

Second, the abusing spouse must not have access to the primary checking account. Obviously, this is where I believe it's appropriate to have separate checking accounts. The reason for joint checking accounts is to experience true financial intimacy in practice, but that was sacrificed when the abusing spouse made their decision to spend inappropriately.

For the abusing spouse I would say this: to have any chance of restoring trust in your marriage, you will need to do exactly what your husband or wife asks of you. If that means you no longer have access to debit cards or cash without their knowledge, so be it. If that means you're expected to provide a detailed report of any money you spend, so be it. You gave up your right to freedom in this area by committing the offense and you have a new set of rules to play by. Through playing by these new rules you have an opportunity to restore the trust that was lost.

To the other spouse I would say this: in spite of the pain caused, you can choose to work through this. If you have a willing heart to manage the entire financial picture and are open to marriage counseling, I believe you can reestablish the relationship with your husband or wife. You will need to open up new bank accounts only in your name and provide funds to your spouse in a monitored manner.

To you both I would say: you made a covenant with each other on your wedding day. You promised to stay with each other for better and for worse. This is for worse. My hope and prayer is that with God's grace you both will seek out the help you need to take back your marriage, and with His help to make it anew.

get naked

thanks

To my mom, Bruce, dad, and Brooke for the encouragement along the way, and the words of wisdom to help me avoid repeating many marital faux pas (and for selling this book to so many people before I was even close to being finished)!

To Sarah for always asking "how's it coming?" and making sure I'm having fun.

To the members of my rogue small group, every time one of you said "I want a signed copy," I knew I had to follow through. Thanks for praying for me, too.

To Christy, your keen eye for design made this book look so much better than I ever could have made it look on my own! To Jon, for marrying Christy, moving to North Carolina, being a great friend, and marking up my draft with red ink.

To Faith for appreciating contractions and creative punctuation, then showing me how to do them better.

To Caleb, Brooke, Mike, and Megan, your friendship is an incredible blessing that I treasure deeply; thanks for loving me for who I am – obsessive compulsive tendencies and all.

To April for allowing me to glean wisdom from your vast knowledge of married people.

To Justin for opening a door to me so that I might do something I can honestly say I love.

To the baristas at the Cary Starbucks and Caribou Coffee for creating a great atmosphere for writing.

To the makers of Mystic Chai, your beverage is quite tasty – like a hug for my insides – at 3:00 AM.

To Rob and Linda for making Elisa, your love, and support.

To Elisa, my lover and best friend. Thank you for your willingness to openly share our story so that others could be blessed and marriages positively changed. I love you!

Dear God, I find myself scratching my head sometimes wondering how I even got to this place. Thank you for your mercy and grace, sense of humor, and patience with this child.

about the author
derek sisterhen

Derek Sisterhen is an author, speaker, and host of the Past Due Radio show (pastdueradio.com).

He's also the Lead Financial Coach at Lukas Coaching where he helps couples establish mutual goals for their money and their lives, and a plan of action for reaching them.

Derek worked in banking as a collections project manager and corporate risk analyst. With a decade of financial experience under his belt, Derek hasn't lost sight of the personal side of personal finance. He loves helping others accomplish what they've only dreamed possible.

Derek and his wife Elisa live in Cary, North Carolina. They're both actively involved with Hope Community Church – you'll find Elisa in the nursery and Derek banging his drums with the band.

You can contact Derek via email at derek@getnakedbook.com.

get naked

stripping down to money and marriage

get naked
LIVE events

Derek speaks in businesses, churches, and other organizations around the country, helping married couples get naked and feel no shame over money. If you'd like to host a Get Naked event, contact booking@getnakedbook.com.

french maid. fireman. marriage. compromise. budgets. money. getting naked. staying naked. unity. intimacy. more sex. less stress. financial differences. game plan. debt. savings. legacy. joy. budget. spending plans. love. engagement. preparation. live events. financial date nights. understanding. no shame. living. freedom. french maid. fireman. marriage. compromise. budgets. money. getting naked. staying naked. unity. intimacy. more sex. less stress. financial differences. game plan. debt. savings. legacy. joy. budget. giving. spending plans. love. engagement. preparation. live events. financial date nights. understanding. no shame. living. freedom. french maid. fireman. marriage. compromise. budgets. money. getting naked. staying naked. unity. intimacy. more sex. less stress. financial differences.